# National Health Service Act 1977

CHAPTER 49

## ARRANGEMENT OF SECTIONS

A

## PART II

### GENERAL MEDICAL, GENERAL DENTAL, GENERAL OPHTHALMIC, AND PHARMACEUTICAL SERVICES

### General medical services

### General dental services

### General ophthalmic services

### Pharmaceutical services

### Local representative committees

### Provisions as to disqualification of practitioners

PART III

OTHER POWERS OF THE SECRETARY OF STATE AS TO
THE HEALTH SERVICE

A 2

*Information and reports*

*Regulations as to certain charges*

*Inquiries, and default and emergency powers*

# PART IV

## PROPERTY AND FINANCE

### *Land and other property*

### *Trusts*

### *Finance and accounts*

ELIZABETH II

# National Health Service Act 1977

## 1977 CHAPTER 49

An Act to consolidate certain provisions relating to the
health service for England and Wales; and to repeal
certain enactments relating to the health service which
have ceased to have any effect.      [29th July 1977]

**B**E IT ENACTED by the Queen's most Excellent Majesty, by and
with the advice and consent of the Lords Spiritual and
Temporal, and Commons, in this present Parliament
assembled, and by the authority of the same, as follows:—

### PART I

#### SERVICES AND ADMINISTRATION

*Functions of the Secretary of State*

1.—(1) It is the Secretary of State's duty to continue the
promotion in England and Wales of a comprehensive health
service designed to secure improvement—

    (*a*) in the physical and mental health of the people of those
countries, and

    (*b*) in the prevention, diagnosis and treatment of illness,

and for that purpose to provide or secure the effective provision
of services in accordance with this Act.

*Secretary of State's duty as to health service.*

(2) The services so provided shall be free of charge except
in so far as the making and recovery of charges is expressly
provided for by or under any enactment, whenever passed.

A 4

PART I
Secretary
of State's
general
power as to
services.

**2.** Without prejudice to the Secretary of State's powers apart from this section, he has power—

(a) to provide such services as he considers appropriate for the purpose of discharging any duty imposed on him by this Act; and

(b) to do any other thing whatsoever which is calculated to facilitate, or is conducive or incidental to, the discharge of such a duty.

This section is subject to section 3(3) below.

Services
generally.

**3.**—(1) It is the Secretary of State's duty to provide throughout England and Wales, to such extent as he considers necessary to meet all reasonable requirements—

(a) hospital accommodation;

(b) other accommodation for the purpose of any service provided under this Act;

(c) medical, dental, nursing and ambulance services;

(d) such other facilities for the care of expectant and nursing mothers and young children as he considers are appropriate as part of the health service;

(e) such facilities for the prevention of illness, the care of persons suffering from illness and the after-care of persons who have suffered from illness as he considers are appropriate as part of the health service;

(f) such other services as are required for the diagnosis and treatment of illness.

1946 c. 81.

(2) Where any hospital provided by the Secretary of State in accordance with this Act was a voluntary hospital transferred by virtue of the National Health Service Act 1946, and—

(a) the character and associations of that hospital before its transfer were such as to link it with a particular religious denomination, then

(b) regard shall be had in the general administration of the hospital to the preservation of that character and those associations.

(3) Nothing in section 2 above or in this section affects the provisions of Part II of this Act (which relates to arrangements with practitioners for the provision of medical, dental, ophthalmic and pharmaceutical services).

Special
hospitals.

1959 c. 72.

**4.** The duty imposed on the Secretary of State by section 1 above to provide services for the purposes of the health service includes a duty to provide and maintain establishments (in this Act referred to as " special hospitals ") for persons subject to detention under the Mental Health Act 1959 who in his opinion require treatment under conditions of special security on account of their dangerous, violent or criminal propensities.

**5.**—(1) It is the Secretary of State's duty—

    (*a*) to provide for the medical and dental inspection at appropriate intervals of pupils in attendance at schools maintained by local education authorities and for the medical and dental treatment of such pupils (and the additional provisions set out in Schedule 1 to this Act have effect in relation to this paragraph) ;

    (*b*) to arrange, to such extent as he considers necessary to meet all reasonable requirements in England and Wales, for the giving of advice on contraception, the medical examination of persons seeking advice on contraception, the treatment of such persons and the supply of contraceptive substances and appliances.

(2) The Secretary of State may—

    (*a*) provide invalid carriages for persons appearing to him to be suffering from severe physical defect or disability and, at the request of such a person, may provide for him a vehicle other than an invalid carriage (and the additional provisions set out in Schedule 2 to this Act have effect in relation to this paragraph) ;

    (*b*) arrange to provide accommodation and treatment outside Great Britain for persons suffering from respiratory tuberculosis ;

    (*c*) provide a microbiological service, which may include the provision of laboratories, for the control of the spread of infectious diseases (and the Secretary of State may allow persons to use services provided at such laboratories on such terms, including terms as to charges, as he thinks fit) ;

    (*d*) conduct, or assist by grants or otherwise (without prejudice to the general powers and duties conferred on him under the Ministry of Health Act 1919) any person to 1919 c. 21. conduct, research into any matters relating to the causation, prevention, diagnosis or treatment of illness, and into any such other matters connected with any service provided under this Act as he considers appropriate.

(3) Regulations may provide for the payment by the Secretary of State in such cases as may be prescribed of travelling expenses (including the travelling expenses of a companion) incurred or to be incurred by persons for the purpose of availing themselves of any services provided under this Act.

(4) The Public Health Laboratory Service Board continues in being for the purpose of exercising such functions with respect to the administration of the public health laboratory service (the service referred to in paragraph (*c*) of subsection (2) above) as the Secretary of State may determine.

(5) The Board shall continue to be constituted in accordance with Part I of Schedule 3 to this Act, and the additional provisions set out in Part II of that Schedule have effect in relation to the Board.

### *Central Health Services Council and Medical Practices Committee*

Central
Health
Services
Council, and
standing
advisory
committees.

**6.**—(1) The Central Health Services Council (in this Act referred to as " the Central Council ") shall have the duty of advising the Secretary of State upon such general matters relating to the services provided under this Act as the Council think fit, and upon any questions relating to those services which he may refer to them.

(2) The Central Council shall be constituted in accordance with Schedule 4 to this Act, but the Secretary of State may by order vary that constitution after consultation with the Council ; and the supplementary provisions of that Schedule have effect in relation to the Central Council and any standing advisory committee constituted under subsection (3) below.

(3) The Secretary of State may, after consultation with the Central Council, by order constitute standing advisory committees for the purpose of advising him and the Council on such of the services provided under this Act as may be specified in the order.

(4) Any committee so constituted shall consist partly of members of the Central Council appointed by the Secretary of State, and partly of persons (whether or not members of the Council) appointed by the Secretary of State after consultation with such representative organisations as he may recognise for the purpose.

(5) It shall be the duty of a committee so constituted to advise the Secretary of State and the Central Council—

   (*a*) upon such matters relating to the services with which the committee are concerned as they think fit, and

   (*b*) upon any questions referred to them by the Secretary of State or the Council relating to those services,

and, if the committee advise the Secretary of State upon any matter, they shall inform the Council, who may express their views on the matter to the Secretary of State.

(6) The Central Council shall make an annual report to the Secretary of State on their proceedings, and on the proceedings of any standing advisory committee constituted under subsection (3) above, and, subject to subsection (7) below, the Secretary of State shall lay that report before Parliament with such comments (if any) as he thinks fit.

(7) If the Secretary of State, after consultation with the Central Council, is satisfied that it would be contrary to the public interest to lay any such report, or a part of any such report before Parliament, he may refrain from so laying that report or that part.

**7.**—(1) The Medical Practices Committee— Medical Practices Committee.

    (*a*) shall consist of a chairman and eight other members appointed by the Secretary of State after consultation with such organisations as he may recognise as representative of the medical profession ; and

    (*b*) the chairman and six of the other members shall be medical practitioners, and five at least of those six shall be actively engaged in medical practice.

(2) The Secretary of State may—

    (*a*) make regulations as to the appointment, tenure of office and vacation of office of the members of the Committee ; and

    (*b*) provide the services of such officers as the Committee may require.

(3) The Committee's proceedings shall not be invalidated by any vacancy in its membership or by any defect in a member's appointment or qualification.

### *Local administration*

**8.**—(1) It is the Secretary of State's duty to establish by Regional and Area Health Authorities. order in accordance with Part I of Schedule 5 to this Act—

    (*a*) authorities, to be called Regional Health Authorities, for such regions in England as he may by order determine, and

    (*b*) authorities, to be called either Area Health Authorities or (in accordance with section 9 below) Area Health Authorities (Teaching), for such areas in Wales and those regions as he may by order determine,

and orders determining regions or areas in pursuance of this subsection shall be separate from orders establishing authorities for the regions or areas.

Any reference in the following provisions of this Act to an Area Health Authority includes a reference to an Area Health Authority (Teaching) unless the context otherwise requires.

(2) The Secretary of State may by order vary the region of a Regional Health Authority or the area of an Area Health Authority whether or not the variation entails the determination of a new or the abolition of an existing region or area.

PART I

(3) It is the Secretary of State's duty to exercise the powers conferred on him by the preceding provisions of this section so as to secure—

> (a) that the regions determined in pursuance of those provisions together comprise the whole of England, that the areas so determined together comprise the whole of Wales and those regions and that no region includes part only of any area ; and

> (b) that the provision of health services in each region can conveniently be associated with a university which has a school of medicine or with two or more such universities.

(4) An order made by virtue of subsection (2) above may (without prejudice to the generality of section 126(4) below) contain such provisions for the transfer of officers, property, rights and liabilities as the Secretary of State thinks fit.

(5) It is the Secretary of State's duty before he makes an order under subsection (2) to consult with respect to the order—

> (a) such bodies as he may recognise as representing officers who in his opinion are likely to be transferred or affected by transfers in pursuance of the order ; and

> (b) such other bodies as he considers are concerned with the order.

Special provisions for Area Health Authorities (Teaching).

**9.**—(1) An order establishing an Authority in pursuance of paragraph (b) of section 8(1) above may provide for it to be called an Area Health Authority (Teaching) if and only if the Secretary of State is satisfied that the Authority is to provide for a university or universities substantial facilities for undergraduate or post-graduate clinical teaching.

(2) Where the Secretary of State is satisfied that an Area Health Authority is to provide, or is providing such facilities, he may provide by order for the Authority to be called an Area Health Authority (Teaching), and, where he is satisfied that an Area Health Authority (Teaching) no longer provides such facilities, he may provide by order for the Authority to be called an Area Health Authority.

(3) It is the Secretary of State's duty, before providing that an Authority shall be called or cease to be called an Area Health Authority (Teaching), to consult the university or universities concerned with the facilities in question.

Family Practitioner Committees.

**10.** It is the duty of each Area Health Authority to establish for its area, in accordance with Part II of Schedule 5 to this Act, a body called a Family Practitioner Committee, and each Family Practitioner Committee has the duty described in section 15 below.

**11.**—(1) If the Secretary of State considers that a special body should be established for the purpose of performing any functions which he may direct the body to perform on his behalf, or on behalf of an Area Health Authority or a Family Practitioner Committee, he may by order establish a body for that purpose.

(2) The Secretary of State may, subject to the provisions of Part III of Schedule 5 to this Act, make such further provision relating to that body as he thinks fit.

(3) A body established in pursuance of this section shall (without prejudice to the power conferred by subsection (4) below to allocate a particular name to the body) be called a special health authority.

(4) Without prejudice to the generality of the power conferred by this section to make an order (or of section 126(4) below), that order may in particular contain provisions as to—

(a) the membership of the body established by the order;

(b) the transfer to the body of officers, property, rights and liabilities; and

(c) the name by which the body is to be known.

(5) It is the Secretary of State's duty before he makes such an order to consult with respect to the order such bodies as he may recognise as representing officers who in his opinion are likely to be transferred or affected by transfers in pursuance of the order.

**12.** The provisions of Part III of Schedule 5 to this Act have effect, so far as applicable, in relation to—

(a) Regional Health Authorities and Area Health Authorities established under section 8 above;

(b) Family Practitioner Committees established under section 10 above;

(c) any special health authority established under section 11 above.

**13.**—(1) The Secretary of State may direct a Regional Health Authority, an Area Health Authority of which the area is in Wales or a special health authority to exercise on his behalf such of his functions relating to the health service as are specified in the directions, and (subject to section 14 below) it shall be the duty of the body in question to comply with the directions.

(2) The Secretary of State's functions under subsection (1) above—

    (*a*) include any of his functions under enactments relating to mental health and nursing homes, but

    (*b*) exclude the duty imposed on him by section 1(1) above to secure the effective provision of the services mentioned in section 15 below.

Regional
Health
Authority's
directions.

**14.**—(1) A Regional Health Authority may direct any Area Health Authority of which the area is included in its region to exercise such of the functions exercisable by the Regional Health Authority by virtue of section 13 above as are specified in the directions, and it is the Area Health Authority's duty to comply with the directions.

(2) If the Secretary of State directs a Regional Health Authority to secure that any of its functions specified in his directions are or are not exercisable by an Area Health Authority it is the Regional Health Authority's duty to comply with his directions.

Duty of
Family
Practitioner
Committee.

**15.**—(1) It is the duty of each Family Practitioner Committee, in accordance with regulations—

    (*a*) to administer, on behalf of the Area Health Authority by which the Committee was established, the arrangements made in pursuance of this Act for the provision of general medical services, general dental services, general ophthalmic services and pharmaceutical services for the area of the Authority, and

    (*b*) to perform such other functions relating to those services as may be prescribed.

(2) If it appears to the Secretary of State that, in consequence of regulations made by virtue of the preceding provisions of this section, references to an Area Health Authority in particular provisions of this Act should be construed as references to a Family Practitioner Committee, he may by regulations provide accordingly.

Exercise of
functions.

**16.**—(1) Regulations may provide for functions exercisable by virtue of the provisions of sections 13 to 15 above by a body other than an Area Health Authority, or exercisable by virtue of any provision of this Act by an Area Health Authority, to be exercisable on behalf of the body in question—

    (*a*) by an equivalent body or by another body of which the members consist only of the body and equivalent bodies ;

(b) by a committee, sub-committee or officer of the body or an equivalent body or such another body as aforesaid ;

(c) in the case of functions exercisable by an Area Health Authority, by a special health authority, an officer of such an authority or a Family Practitioner Committee ;

(d) in the case of functions exercisable by a Family Practitioner Committee, by a special health authority, an officer of such an authority or an officer of an Area Health Authority.

(2) For the purposes of subsection (1) above, a Regional or Area Health Authority or a Family Practitioner Committee is equivalent to another body of the same name and a special health authority is equivalent to another such authority.

(3) Nothing in this section shall be construed as precluding any body from acting by an agent where it is entitled so to act apart from this section.

**17.** The Secretary of State may give directions with respect to Directions as the exercise of any functions exercisable by virtue of sections 13 to exercise to 16 above, or by an Area Health Authority by virtue of Part II of functions. of this Act ; and, subject to any directions given by the Secretary of State by virtue of this section—

(a) a Regional Health Authority may give directions with respect to the exercise by an Area Health Authority of which the area is included in its region, of any functions exercisable by the Area Health Authority by virtue of section 14 above,

(b) an Area Health Authority may give directions with respect to the exercise by the Family Practitioner Committee established by it of any functions which are exercisable by the Committee by virtue of section 15 above and are prescribed for the purposes of this paragraph,

and it shall be the duty of the body in question to comply with the directions.

**18.**—(1) Any directions given by the Secretary of State in Directions pursuance of sections 13 to 17 above shall be given either by under regulations or by an instrument in writing, except that— generally.

(a) any such directions in pursuance of section 13 above in respect of functions relating to special hospitals, and

(b) any such directions in respect of functions conferred on the Secretary of State by section 20(1) or (2) below,

shall only be given by regulations.

(2) Any directions given by an Authority in pursuance of sections 13 to 17 shall be given by an instrument in writing.

(3) Directions given and regulations made under sections 13 to 17 in respect of any function—

(*a*) shall not, except in prescribed cases, preclude a body or person by whom the function is exercisable apart from the directions or regulations from exercising the function, and

(*b*) may in the case of directions given by an instrument in writing be varied or revoked by subsequent directions given in pursuance of those sections and this section (without prejudice to the operation of section 32(3) of the Interpretation Act 1889 in the case of directions given by regulations),

1889 c. 63.

so, however, that an Area Health Authority shall not be entitled to exercise any functions which, by virtue of section 15 above, are exercisable by the Family Practitioner Committee established by the Authority.

*Local advisory committees and
Community Health Councils*

Local
advisory
committees.

**19.**—(1) Where the Secretary of State is satisfied that a committee formed for Wales, or for the region of a Regional Health Authority, is representative of persons of any of the following categories—

(*a*) the medical practitioners, or

(*b*) the dental practitioners, or

(*c*) the nurses and midwives, or

(*d*) the registered pharmacists, or

(*e*) the ophthalmic and dispensing opticians,

of Wales or of the region, then it shall be his duty to recognise the committee.

(2) A committee recognised in pursuance of subsection (1) above shall be called—

(*a*) the Welsh Medical, Dental, Nursing and Midwifery, Pharmaceutical or Optical Committee, as the case may be ;

(*b*) the Regional Medical, Dental, Nursing and Midwifery, Pharmaceutical or Optical Committee, as the case may be, for the region in question.

(3) Where the Secretary of State is satisfied that a committee formed for the area of an Area Health Authority is representative of persons of any of the categories mentioned in paragraphs

(*a*) to (*e*) in subsection (1) it shall be his duty to recognise the PART I committee.

A committee recognised in pursuance of this subsection shall be called the Area Medical, Dental, Nursing and Midwifery, Pharmaceutical or Optical Committee, as the case may be, for the area in question.

(4) The Secretary of State's duty under subsections (1) and (3) above is subject to paragraph 1 of Schedule 6 to this Act, and that Schedule has effect in relation to a committee recognised in pursuance of this section.

**20.**—(1) It is the Secretary of State's duty to establish in Community accordance with this section a council for the area of each Area Health Health Authority, or separate councils for such separate parts Councils. of the areas of those Authorities as he thinks fit, and such a council shall be called a Community Health Council.

(2) The Secretary of State—

(*a*) may if he thinks fit discharge this duty by establishing a Community Health Council for a district which includes the areas or parts of the areas of two or more Area Health Authorities, but

(*b*) shall be treated as not having discharged that duty unless he secures that there is no part of the area of an Area Health Authority which is not included in some Community Health Council's district.

(3) The additional provisions of Schedule 7 to this Act have effect in relation to Community Health Councils.

### Co-operation and assistance

**21.**—(1) Subject to paragraphs (*d*) and (*e*) of section 3(1) Local social above, the services described in Schedule 8 to this Act in relation services to— authorities.

(*a*) care of mothers and young children,

(*b*) prevention, care and after-care,

(*c*) home help and laundry facilities,

are functions exercisable by local social services authorities, and that Schedule has effect accordingly.

(2) A local social services authority who provide premises, furniture or equipment for any of the purposes of this Act may permit the use of the premises, furniture or equipment—

(*a*) by any other local social services authority, or

(*b*) by any of the bodies constituted under this Act, or

(*c*) by a local education authority.

This permission may be on such terms (including terms with respect to the services of any staff employed by the authority giving permission) as may be agreed.

(3) A local social services authority may provide (or improve or furnish) residential accommodation—

> (*a*) for officers employed by them for the purposes of any of their functions as a local social services authority, or
> (*b*) for officers employed by a voluntary organisation for the purposes of any services provided under this section and Schedule 8.

Co-operation between health authorities and local authorities.

**22.**—(1) In exercising their respective functions health authorities and local authorities shall co-operate with one another in order to secure and advance the health and welfare of the people of England and Wales.

(2) There shall be committees, to be called joint consultative committees, who shall advise Area Health Authorities and the authorities in column 2 of the Table below on the performance of their duties under subsection (1) above, and on the planning and operation of services of common concern to those authorities.

TABLE

| 1<br>*Area Health Authority* | 2<br>*Associated authorities* |
|---|---|
| An Area Health Authority in a metropolitan county in England. | The local authority for each district wholly or partly in the area of the Authority. |
| An Area Health Authority in a non-metropolitan county in England, or an Area Health Authority in Wales. | The local authority for each county, and also for each district, wholly or partly in the area of the Authority. |
| An Area Health Authority in Greater London. | The local authority for each London borough wholly or partly in the area of the Authority.<br>Also the Inner London Education Authority, if wholly or partly in the area of the Authority.<br>Also the Common Council of the City of London, if in the area of the Authority. |

(3) Except as provided by an order under the following provisions of this section, each joint consultative committee shall represent one or more Area Health Authorities together with

one or more of the authorities in column 2 of the Table above, and an Area Health Authority shall be represented together with each of the authorities associated with that Authority in column 2 of the said Table in one or other of the committees (but not necessarily the same committee).

(4) The Secretary of State shall have power by order to provide for any matter relating to joint consultative committees, and such an order may in particular—

(a) provide for the way in which the provisions of subsections (2) and (3) above are to be carried out, or provide for varying the arrangements set out in those subsections ;

(b) provide, where it appears to the Secretary of State appropriate, for an Area Health Authority to be represented on a joint consultative committee together with a local or other authority whose area is not within the area of the Area Health Authority ;

(c) afford a choice to any authorities as to the number of joint consultative committees on which they are to be represented, and provide for the case where the authorities cannot agree on the choice ;

(d) authorise or require a joint consultative committee to appoint any sub-committee or to join with another joint consultative committee or other joint consultative committees in appointing a joint sub-committee ;

(e) authorise or require the appointment to a joint consultative committee, or to any sub-committee, of persons who are not members of the authorities represented by the joint consultative committee ;

(f) require the authorities represented on a joint consultative committee to defray the expenses of the committee, and of any sub-committee, in such shares as may be determined by or under the order, and provide for the way in which any dispute between those authorities concerning the expenses is to be resolved ; and

(g) require those authorities to make reports to the Secretary of State on the work of the joint consultative committee and of any sub-committee.

(5) Before making an order under this section the Secretary of State shall consult with such associations of local authorities as appear to him to be concerned, and with any local authority with whom consultation appears to him to be desirable.

**23.**—(1) The Secretary of State may, where he considers it Voluntary appropriate, arrange with any person or body (including a volun- organisations tary organisation) for that person or body to provide, or assist and other in providing, any service under this Act. bodies.

In this section "voluntary organisation" means a body the activities of which are carried on otherwise than for profit, but does not include any public or local authority.

(2) The Secretary of State may make available—

> (*a*) to any person or body (including a voluntary organisation) carrying out any arrangements under subsection (1) above, or

1968 c. 46.
> (*b*) to any voluntary organisation eligible for assistance under section 64 or section 65 of the Health Services and Public Health Act 1968 (assistance made available by the Secretary of State or local authorities),

any facilities (including goods or materials, or the use of any premises and the use of any vehicle, plant or apparatus) provided by him for any service under this Act ; and, where anything is so made available, the services of persons employed by the Secretary of State or by a health authority in connection with it.

(3) The powers conferred by this section may be exercised on such terms as may be agreed, including terms as to the making of payments by or to the Secretary of State, and any goods or materials may be made available either temporarily or permanently.

(4) The Secretary of State may by order provide that, in relation to a vehicle which is made available by him in pursuance of this section and is used in accordance with the terms on which it is so made available, the Vehicles (Excise) Act 1971 and
1971 c. 10.
1972 c. 20.
Part VI of the Road Traffic Act 1972 shall have effect with such modifications as are specified in the order.

(5) Any power to supply goods or materials conferred by this section includes a power to purchase and store them and includes a power to arrange with third parties for the supply of goods or materials by those third parties.

Overseas
aid.
**24.** Each health authority and the Public Health Laboratory Service Board has power—

> (*a*) with the Secretary of State's consent, to enter into and carry out agreements with the relevant Minister under which, at the expense of that Minister, the authority or board acts as the instrument by means of which he furnishes technical assistance in the exercise of the
1966 c. 21.
> power conferred on him by section 1(1) of the Overseas Aid Act 1966 ;

> (*b*) with the consent of the Secretary of State and the relevant Minister, to enter into and carry out agreements which under the authority or board furnishes, for any

purpose specified in that section 1(1), technical assis- tance (excluding financial assistance) in any country or territory outside the United Kingdom against reimbursement to the authority or board of the cost of furnishing the assistance.

In this section " the relevant Minister " means the Minister of the Crown by whom is exercisable the power conferred on the Minister of Overseas Development by that section 1(1) as originally enacted.

**25.** Where the Secretary of State has acquired— Supplies not

readily
(a) supplies of human blood for the purposes of any service obtainable. under this Act, or

(b) any part of a human body for the purpose of, or in the course of providing, any such service, or

(c) supplies of any other substances or preparations not readily obtainable,

he may arrange to make such supplies or that part available (on such terms, including terms as to charges, as he thinks fit) to any person.

This section is subject to section 62 below (restriction of powers under sections 25, 58 and 61).

**26.**—(1) The Secretary of State may— Supply of

(a) supply to local authorities, and to such public bodies goods and
services by
or classes of public bodies as he may determine, any Secretary goods or materials of a kind used in the health service ; of State.

(b) make available to local authorities, and to those bodies or classes of bodies, any facilities (including the use of any premises and the use of any vehicle, plant or apparatus) provided by him for any service under this Act, and the services of persons employed by the Secretary of State or by a health authority ;

(c) carry out maintenance work in connection with any land or building for the maintenance of which a local authority is responsible.

In this subsection—

" maintenance work " includes minor renewals, minor improvements and minor extensions ; and

" public bodies " includes public bodies in Northern Ireland.

(2) The Secretary of State may supply or make available to persons providing general medical services, general dental services, general ophthalmic services or pharmaceutical services such goods, materials or other facilities as may be prescribed.

(3) The Secretary of State shall make available to local authorities—

(a) any services or other facilities (excluding the services of any person but including goods or materials, the use of any premises and the use of any vehicle, plant or apparatus) provided under this Act,

(b) the services provided as part of the health service by any person employed by the Secretary of State or a health authority, and

(c) the services of any medical practitioner, dental practitioner or nurse employed by the Secretary of State or a health authority otherwise than to provide services which are part of the health service,

so far as is reasonably necessary and practicable to enable local authorities to discharge their functions relating to social services, education and public health.

Conditions
of supply
under s. 26.

**27.**—(1) It is the Secretary of State's duty, before he makes the services of any officer of a health authority available in pursuance of subsection (1)(b) or subsection (3)(b) or (c) of section 26 above, to consult the officer or a body recognised by the Secretary of State as representing the officer about the matter, or to satisfy himself that the health authority has consulted the officer about the matter.

(2) The Secretary of State shall be entitled to disregard the provisions of subsection (1) above in a case where he considers it necessary to make the services of an officer available as mentioned in that subsection for the purpose of dealing temporarily with an emergency, and has previously consulted such a body about the making available of services in an emergency.

(3) For the purposes of subsection (1)(b) or subsection (3)(b) or (c) of section 26 the Secretary of State may give such directions to health authorities to make the services of their officers available as he considers appropriate ; and it shall be the health authority's duty to comply with any such directions.

(4) The powers conferred by this section and section 26 may be exercised on such terms as may be agreed, including terms as to the making of payments to the Secretary of State, and such charges may be made by the Secretary of State in respect of services or facilities provided under subsection (3) of section 26 as may be agreed between the Secretary of State and the local

authority or, in default of agreement, as may be determined by arbitration.

PART I

(5) The Secretary of State may by order provide that, in relation to a vehicle which is made available by him in pursuance of section 26 and is used in accordance with the terms on which it is so made available, the Vehicles (Excise) Act 1971 and Part VI of the Road Traffic Act 1972 shall have effect with such modifications as are specified in the order.

1971 c. 10.
1972 c. 20.

(6) Any power to supply goods or materials conferred by section 26 includes a power to purchase and store them, and a power to arrange with third parties for the supply of goods or materials by those third parties.

**28.**—(1) In the Local Authorities (Goods and Services) Act 1970 the expression " public body " includes any health authority and so far as relates to his functions under this Act includes the Secretary of State.

Supply of goods and services by local authorities.
1970 c. 39.

(2) The provisions of subsection (1) above have effect as if made by an order under section 1(5) of that Act of 1970, and accordingly may be varied or revoked by such an order.

(3) Every local authority shall make available to health authorities acting in the area of the local authority the services of persons employed by the local authority for the purposes of the local authority's functions under the Local Authorities Social Services Act 1970 so far as is reasonably necessary and practicable to enable health authorities to discharge their functions under this Act.

1970 c. 42.

(4) Such charges may be made by a local authority for acting under subsection (3) above as may be agreed between the local authority and the Secretary of State or, in default of agreement, as may be determined by arbitration.

## PART II

### GENERAL MEDICAL, GENERAL DENTAL, GENERAL OPHTHALMIC, AND PHARMACEUTICAL SERVICES

#### *General medical services*

**29.**—(1) It is every Area Health Authority's duty, in accordance with regulations, to arrange as respects their area with medical practitioners to provide personal medical services for all persons in the area who wish to take advantage of the arrangements.

Arrangements and regulations for general medical services.

The services so provided are in this Act referred to as " general medical services ".

(2) Regulations may provide for the definition of the personal medical services to be provided and for securing that the arrangements will be such that all persons availing themselves of those services will receive adequate personal care and attendance, and the regulations shall include provision—

(a) for the preparation and publication of lists of medical practitioners who undertake to provide general medical services ;

(b) for conferring a right on any person to choose, in accordance with the prescribed procedure, the medical practitioner by whom he is to be attended, subject to the consent of the practitioner so chosen and to any prescribed limit on the number of patients to be accepted by any practitioner ;

(c) for the distribution among medical practitioners whose names are on the lists of any persons who have indicated a wish to obtain general medical services but who have not made any choice of medical practitioner or have been refused by the practitioner chosen ;

(d) for the issue to patients or their personal representatives by medical practitioners providing those services of such certificates as may be prescribed being certificates reasonably required by them under or for the purposes of any enactment ;

(e) for the removal from the list of medical practitioners undertaking to provide general medical services for persons in any area of the name of any one in whose case it has been determined in such manner as may be prescribed that he has never provided, or has ceased to provide, such general medical services for persons in that area.

(3) Regulations under subsection (2) above may provide for the personal medical services there mentioned to include the provision of, and services connected with, any such advice, examination and treatment as are mentioned in paragraph (b) of section 5(1) above.

(4) The remuneration to be paid under the arrangements mentioned in subsection (1) above to a practitioner who provides general medical services shall not, except in special circumstances, consist wholly or mainly of a fixed salary which has no reference to the number of patients for whom he has undertaken to provide such services.

**30.**—(1) All applications made in the prescribed manner to an Area Health Authority for inclusion in a list kept by that Authority of the names of medical practitioners undertaking to provide general medical services for persons in the Authority's area shall be referred by the Authority to the Medical Practices Committee and (except as mentioned in subsection (2) below) any medical practitioner whose application is granted by that Committee shall be entitled to the inclusion of his name in the list.

(2) That entitlement is subject to—

    (a) if the Secretary of State should so prescribe, section 31 below ;

    (b) section 33 below (distribution of general medical services);

    (c) section 46 below (disqualification of practitioners).

**31.**—(1) Where the Secretary of State so prescribes, and after a day so prescribed—

    (a) the Medical Practices Committee shall refuse any application under section 30 above if the medical practitioner is not suitably experienced ; and

    (b) an Area Health Authority shall not arrange under section 29 above with a medical practitioner for him to provide general medical services for persons in its area unless the Medical Practices Committee have granted an application by him for the inclusion of his name in the list kept by the Authority of medical practitioners undertaking to provide general medical services for persons in that area.

(2) For the purposes of this section a medical practitioner is " suitably experienced " if, but only if, he either—

    (a) has acquired the prescribed medical experience, or

    (b) is by virtue of regulations made under section 32 below exempt from the need to have acquired that experience,

and " medical experience " includes hospital experience in any specialty.

**32.**—(1) Regulations may for the purposes of section 31 above provide—

    (a) for prescribing the medical experience needed to satisfy paragraph (a) of section 31(2) ;

(*b*) as to the documents which an applicant may or must produce as evidence that he is suitably experienced or has acquired medical experience of any particular kind ;

(*c*) for requiring an applicant who claims to have acquired the prescribed experience to submit particulars of his experience to a prescribed body, and for requiring that body, if satisfied that he has acquired the prescribed experience, to issue him a certificate (a " certificate of prescribed experience ") to that effect ;

(*d*) for enabling an applicant without the prescribed experience who considers that the medical experience which he has acquired is, or ought to be regarded as, equivalent to the prescribed experience to submit particulars of that experience to a prescribed body, and for requiring or enabling that body, if satisfied that the applicant's medical experience is so equivalent, to issue him a certificate (a " certificate of equivalent experience ") to that effect ;

(*e*) for treating an applicant who holds a certificate of equivalent experience as satisfying paragraph (*a*) of section 31(2) ;

(*f*) as to the circumstances or conditions in or subject to which a medical practitioner is exempt from the need to have acquired the prescribed experience ;

(*g*) for conferring on an applicant who is refused a certificate of prescribed experience or a certificate of equivalent experience a right of appeal to a body constituted by the Secretary of State, and for any matter for which it appears to the Secretary of State to be requisite or expedient to provide in consequence of the conferring of that right ;

(*h*) for anything authorised or required by section 31 to be prescribed or otherwise provided for by regulations.

In this section—

" applicant " means a medical practitioner who has made or proposes to make an application to which paragraph (*a*) of section 31(1) applies ;

" the prescribed experience " means the medical experience for the time being prescribed for the purposes of paragraph (*a*) of section 31 (2).

(2) Regulations under this section shall be framed so as to allow the prescribed experience to be acquired without undertaking whole-time employment.

(3) Any power under this section to make regulations—

(a) may be exercised so as to make different provision for different areas or different periods of time or in relation to different cases or different circumstances;

(b) includes power to make such incidental or supplemental provision in the regulations as the Secretary of State considers appropriate.

**33.**—(1) The Medical Practices Committee may refuse any Distribution application under section 30 above on the ground that the of general number of medical practitioners undertaking to provide general medical medical services in the area of the Area Health Authority services. concerned or in part of that area is already adequate.

(2) If in the opinion of the Medical Practices Committee additional practitioners are required for any area or part, but the number of applications exceeds the number required, the Committee shall select the persons whose applications are to be granted and shall refuse the other applications.

(3) Before selecting any persons under subsection (2) above the Medical Practices Committee shall consult the Area Health Authority concerned, and that Authority shall, if a local medical committee has been formed for that Authority's area and recognised under section 44 below, consult that local medical committee before expressing their views on the persons to be selected.

(4) Except as provided in subsections (1) to (3) above, or as required by section 31 above, the Medical Practices Committee shall not refuse any application under section 30, but the Committee may grant an application subject to conditions excluding the provision of general medical services by the applicant in such part or parts of the area of the Area Health Authority as the Committee may specify.

(5) A medical practitioner who has made an application under section 30 which has been refused or has been granted subject to such conditions may appeal to the Secretary of State; and the Secretary of State may, on any such appeal, direct the Medical Practices Committee to grant the application either unconditionally or subject to such conditions as the Secretary of State may specify.

This subsection does not apply where an application has been refused under paragraph (a) of section 31(1).

(6) Where the Medical Practices Committee select persons from a number of applicants, the persons selected shall not be included in the list in question during the period for bringing

an appeal to the Secretary of State or pending the determination of any such appeal.

(7) If the Secretary of State grants an appeal to which subsection (6) above relates, he may direct either that the application—

(a) shall be granted in addition to those already granted ; or

(b) shall be granted instead of such one of those applications as he may specify.

In the latter case, he shall make the other applicant a party to the appeal, and no further appeal shall be brought by that applicant in respect of the application in question.

(8) The Medical Practices Committee shall, in a case where persons have to be selected from a number of applicants, and the Secretary of State shall on an appeal in any such case—

(a) have regard to any desire expressed by any applicant to practise with other medical practitioners already providing general medical services in the area or part of an area concerned and of any desire expressed by such other practitioners to take any applicant into practice with them ;

(b) have special regard to such matters in cases where an applicant is related to any other such practitioner.

Regulations for Medical Practices Committee.

**34.** Regulations may make provisions for conferring or imposing on the Medical Practices Committee such additional functions in relation to arrangements for the provision of general medical services as may be prescribed ; and regulations shall provide—

(a) for requiring Area Health Authorities to make to the Medical Practices Committee, at such times and in such manner as may be prescribed, reports as to—

(i) the number of medical practitioners required to meet the reasonable needs of their areas and the different parts of those areas ;

(ii) the occurrence of any vacancies on the lists of medical practitioners kept by them under this Part of this Act ; and

(iii) the need for filling such vacancies ; and

(b) for prescribing the procedure for—

(i) the determination of applications by the Medical Practices Committee ;

(ii) the making and determination of appeals to the Secretary of State under section 33 above ; and

(iii) requiring Area Health Authorities and applicants to be informed of the decisions of the Committee and the Secretary of State.

## General dental services

**35.**—(1) It is every Area Health Authority's duty, in accordance with regulations, to make as respects their area arrangements with dental practitioners under which any person in the area for whom a dental practitioner undertakes in accordance with the arrangements to provide dental treatment and appliances shall receive such treatment and appliances.

*Arrangements for general dental services.*

The services so provided are in this Act referred to as " general dental services ".

(2) The remuneration to be paid under such arrangements to a dental practitioner who provides general dental services elsewhere than at a health centre shall not consist wholly or mainly of a fixed salary unless either—

(a) the remuneration is paid in pursuance of arrangements made under section 56 below, or

(b) the services are provided in prescribed circumstances and the practitioner consents,

and it shall be the Secretary of State's duty, before he prescribes any circumstances for the purposes of paragraph (b), to consult such organisations as appear to him to be representative of the dental profession.

**36.** Regulations may provide as to the arrangements to be made under section 35 above, and shall include provision—

*Regulations as to s. 35.*

(a) for the preparation and publication of lists of dental practitioners who undertake to provide general dental services ;

(b) for conferring a right, subject to the provisions of this Part of this Act relating to the disqualification of practitioners, on any dental practitioner, who wishes to be included in any such list, to be so included ;

(c) for conferring on any person a right to choose, in accordance with the prescribed procedure, the dental practitioner from whom he is to receive general dental services, subject to the consent of the practitioner so chosen ;

(d) for the removal from the list of dental practitioners undertaking to provide general dental services for persons in any area of the name of any one in whose case it has been determined in such manner as may be prescribed that he has never provided, or has ceased to provide, such general dental services for persons in that area.

**37.** Regulations providing as to the arrangements to be made under section 35 above shall include provision—

*Dental Estimates Board.*

(a) for constituting a Board, to be called the Dental Estimates Board, of whom the chairman and a majority of the members shall be dental practitioners, for the purpose of carrying out such duties as may be prescribed with respect to the approval of estimates of dental treatment and appliances, and to the remuneration of dental practitioners providing general dental services;

(b) for providing in relation to that Board for any of the matters for which, in relation to an Area Health Authority, provision is or may be made by or under Part III of Schedule 5 to this Act.

### General ophthalmic services

**38.** It is every Area Health Authority's duty, in accordance with regulations, to arrange as respects their area with medical practitioners having the prescribed qualifications, ophthalmic opticians, and dispensing opticians for securing the testing of sight by such medical practitioners and ophthalmic opticians, and the supply by ophthalmic opticians and dispensing opticians of optical appliances.

The services so provided are in this Act referred to as " general ophthalmic services ".

**39.** Regulations may provide as to the arrangements to be made under section 38 above, and shall include provision—

(a) for the preparation and publication of lists of medical practitioners, ophthalmic opticians and dispensing opticians, respectively, who undertake to provide general ophthalmic services;

(b) for conferring a right, subject to the provisions of this Act relating to the disqualification of practitioners, on any medical practitioner having the prescribed qualifications, ophthalmic optician or dispensing optician who wishes to be included in the appropriate list, to be so included;

(c) for conferring on any person a right to choose in accordance with the prescribed procedure the medical practitioner or ophthalmic optician by whom his sight is to be tested, or from whom any prescription for the supply of optical appliances is to be obtained and the ophthalmic or dispensing optician who wishes to supply the appliances;

(d) for the removal from the list of medical practitioners, ophthalmic opticians or dispensing opticians undertaking to provide general ophthalmic services for persons in any area of the name of any one in whose case it has been determined in such manner as may be prescribed that he has never provided, or has ceased to provide, such general ophthalmic services for persons in that area.

**40.** The power conferred by section 38 above (in relation to general ophthalmic services) to prescribe the qualifications to be possessed by any medical practitioner includes a power—

(*a*) to prescribe a requirement that the practitioner shall show to the satisfaction of a committee recognised by the Secretary of State for the purpose that he possesses such qualifications, including qualifications as to experience, as may be mentioned in the regulations; and

(*b*) to confer on a person who is dissatisfied with the determination of such a committee, a right of appeal to a committee appointed by the Secretary of State, and to provide for any matter for which it appears to the Secretary of State to be requisite or expedient to provide in consequence of the conferring of that right.

### Pharmaceutical services

**41.** It is every Area Health Authority's duty, in accordance with regulations, to arrange as respects their area for the supply to persons who are in that area of—

(*a*) proper and sufficient drugs and medicines and listed appliances which are ordered for those persons by a medical practitioner in pursuance of his functions in the health service, the Scottish health service, the Northern Ireland health service or the armed forces of the Crown (excluding forces of a Commonwealth country and forces raised in a colony); and

(*b*) listed drugs and medicines which are ordered for those persons by a dental practitioner in pursuance of such functions.

The services so provided are in this Act referred to as " pharmaceutical services ".

In this section—

" listed " means included in a list for the time being approved by the Secretary of State for the purposes of this section ; and

" the Scottish health service " and " the Northern Ireland health service " mean respectively the health service established in pursuance of section 1 of the National Health Service (Scotland) Act 1947 or any service provided in pursuance of Article 4(*a*) of the Health and Personal Social Services (Northern Ireland) Order 1972.

**42.** Regulations may provide for securing that arrangements made under section 41 above will be such as to enable any person for whom they are ordered as mentioned in that section

PART II    to receive the drugs, medicines and appliances there mentioned
from any person with whom such arrangements have been
made ; and the regulations shall include provision—

> (a) for the preparation and publication of lists of persons
> who undertake to provide pharmaceutical services ;
>
> (b) for conferring a right, subject to this Part of this Act
> relating to the disqualification of practitioners, on any
> person who wishes to be included in any such list to
> be so included for the purpose of supplying such
> drugs, medicines and appliances as that person is
> entitled by law to sell ; and
>
> (c) for the removal from the list of persons undertaking
> to provide pharmaceutical services for persons in any
> area of the name of any one in whose case it has
> been determined in such manner as may be prescribed
> that he has never provided, or has ceased to provide,
> such pharmaceutical services for persons in that area.

Persons
authorised to
provide
pharmaceutical
services.

**43.**—(1) No arrangements shall be made by an Area Health
Authority (except as may be provided by regulations) with a
medical practitioner or dental practitioner under which he is
required or agrees to provide pharmaceutical services to any
person to whom he is rendering general medical services or
general dental services.

1968 c. 67.

(2) No arrangements for the dispensing of medicines shall be
made (except as may be provided by regulations) with persons
other than persons who are registered pharmacists, or are
persons lawfully conducting a retail pharmacy business in
accordance with section 69 of the Medicines Act 1968 and who
undertake that all medicines supplied by them under the
arrangements made under this Part of this Act shall be dispensed
either by or under the direct supervision of a registered pharmacist.

## *Local representative committees*

Recognition
of local
representative
committees.

**44.**—(1) Where the Secretary of State is satisfied that a
committee formed for the area of any Area Health Authority
is representative—

> (a) of the medical practitioners providing general medical
> services or general ophthalmic services in that area, or
>
> (b) of the dental practitioners providing general dental
> services in that area, or
>
> (c) of the ophthalmic opticians and dispensing opticians
> providing general ophthalmic services in that area, or
>
> (d) of the persons providing pharmaceutical services in that
> area,

he may recognise that committee ; and any committee so recognised shall be called the Local Medical Committee, the Local
Dental Committee, the Local Optical Committee or the Local
Pharmaceutical Committee, as the case may be, for the
area concerned.

(2) Any such committee may with the Secretary of State's
approval delegate any of their functions, with or without
restrictions or conditions, to sub-committees composed of
members of that committee.

**45.**—(1) The Family Practitioner Committee for the area of Functions of
an Area Health Authority in respect of which committees are local
recognised under section 44 above shall, in exercising their representative
functions under this Part of this Act, consult with those com- committees.
mittees on such occasions and to such extent as may be
prescribed ; and those committees shall exercise such other
functions as may be prescribed.

(2) The Family Practitioner Committee may, on the request
of any committee recognised under section 44 for their area,
allot to that committee such sums for defraying the committee's
administrative expenses (including travelling and subsistence
allowances payable to its members) as may be determined by
the Family Practitioner Committee with the Secretary of State's
approval.

(3) Any sums so allotted shall be out of the moneys available
to the Family Practitioner Committee for the remuneration of
persons of whom the committee so recognised is representative
and who provide general medical services, general dental
services, general ophthalmic services or pharmaceutical services,
as the case may be, under this Part of this Act.

The amount of any such sums shall be deducted from the
remuneration of those persons in such manner as may be
determined by the Family Practitioner Committee with the
Secretary of State's approval.

*Provisions as to disqualification of practitioners*

**46.**—(1) There shall be a tribunal (in this section and sections Disqualifica-
47 to 49 below referred to as " the Tribunal ") which shall be tion of
constituted in accordance with Schedule 9 to this Act to inquire practitioners.
into cases where representations are made in the prescribed
manner to the Tribunal by an Area Health Authority or any
other person that the continued inclusion of a person's name in
a list prepared under this Part of this Act—

> (a) of medical practitioners undertaking to provide general
> medical services,

B

    (b) of medical practitioners undertaking to provide general ophthalmic services,

    (c) of dental practitioners undertaking to provide general dental services,

    (d) of ophthalmic opticians undertaking to provide general ophthalmic services,

    (e) of dispensing opticians undertaking to provide general ophthalmic services, or

    (f) of persons undertaking to provide pharmaceutical services,

would be prejudicial to the efficiency of the services in question.

The supplementary provisions contained in Schedule 9 apply in relation to the Tribunal.

(2) The Tribunal, on receiving representations from an Area Health Authority shall, and in any other case may, inquire into the case, and, if they are of opinion that the continued inclusion of that person's name in any list to which the representations relate would be prejudicial to the efficiency of those services—

    (a) shall direct that his name be removed from that list; and

    (b) may also, if they think fit, direct that his name be removed from, or not be included in, any corresponding list kept by any other Area Health Authority under this Part.

(3) An appeal shall lie to the Secretary of State from any direction of the Tribunal under subsection (2) above, and the Secretary of State may confirm or revoke that direction.

(4) Where the Tribunal direct that the name of any person be removed from or not included in any list or lists the Area Health Authority or Authorities concerned shall—

    (a) if no appeal is brought, at the end of the period for bringing an appeal, or

    (b) if an appeal is brought and the decision of the Tribunal is confirmed by the Secretary of State, on receiving notice of the Secretary of State's decision,

remove the name of the person concerned from the list or lists in question.

Removal of disqualification.

**47.**—(1) Any person whose name has been removed by a direction under section 46 above from any list or lists shall be disqualified for inclusion in any list to which that direction relates until the Tribunal or the Secretary of State direct under this section to the contrary.

(2) For the purpose of deciding whether or not to issue a direction under this section (or under paragraph 8 of Schedule 14 to this Act), the Tribunal or the Secretary of State, as the case may be, may hold an inquiry.

PART II

**48.** Where—

(a) under any provisions in force in Scotland or Northern Ireland corresponding to the provisions of this Part of this Act a person is for the time being disqualified for inclusion in all lists prepared under those provisions of persons undertaking to provide services of one or more of the kinds specified in section 46(1) above, then

(b) that person shall, so long as that disqualification is in force, be disqualified for inclusion in a list prepared under this Part of persons undertaking to provide services of those kinds, and the name of that person shall be removed from every such list in which his name is included.

Disqualification provisions in Scotland or Northern Ireland.

**49.** Regulations shall provide—

(a) for prescribing the procedure for the holding of inquiries by the Tribunal or the Secretary of State under sections 46 to 48 above, and for the making and determining of appeals to the Secretary of State under that procedure, and, in particular for securing that any person who is the subject of such an inquiry shall have an opportunity—

(i) of appearing, either in person or by counsel or solicitor or such other representative as may be prescribed, before the Tribunal and, in the case of an inquiry by, or appeal to, the Secretary of State before a person appointed by the Secretary of State, and

(ii) of being heard by the Tribunal or the person so appointed and of calling witnesses and producing other evidence on his behalf,

and that the hearing, whether by the Tribunal or the person so appointed shall be in public if the person who is the subject of the inquiry so requests ;

(b) for conferring on the Tribunal and on any person so appointed such powers as the Secretary of State considers necessary, and for that purpose to apply, with any necessary modifications, any of the provisions of section 250 of the Local Government Act 1972 ; and

(c) for the publication of the decisions of the Tribunal and the Secretary of State under this section and of

Regulations as to ss. 46 to 48.

1972 c. 70.

PART II     the imposition and removal of any disqualifications imposed under section 48 above.

*Other provisions supplementary to Part II*

Exercise of choice of practitioner in certain cases.     **50.** Regulations may provide that, where a right to choose the person by whom services are to be provided under this Part of this Act is conferred by or under this Part, that right shall, in the case of such persons as may be specified in the regulations, be exercised on their behalf by other persons so specified.

University clinical teaching and research.     **51.** It is the Secretary of State's duty to make available, in premises provided by him by virtue of this Act, such facilities as he considers are reasonably required by any university which has a medical or dental school, in connection with clinical teaching and with research connected with clinical medicine or, as the case may be, clinical dentistry.

Use of accommodation.     **52.** If the Secretary of State considers that any accommodation provided by him by virtue of this Act is suitable for use in connection with the provision of general medical services, general dental services, general ophthalmic services or pharmaceutical services he may make the accommodation available on such terms as he thinks fit to persons providing any of those services.

Immunisation.     **53.** Where the Secretary of State arranges with medical practitioners for the vaccination or immunisation of persons against disease, he shall so far as reasonably practicable give every medical practitioner providing general medical services an opportunity to participate in the arrangements.

Prohibition of sale of medical practices.     **54.**—(1) Where the name of any medical practitioner is or has been at any time entered on any list of medical practitioners undertaking to provide general medical services, it shall be unlawful subsequently to sell the goodwill or any part of the goodwill of the medical practice of that medical practitioner.

This subsection is subject to subsections (2) and (3) below ; and the additional provisions contained in Schedule 10 to this Act have effect for the purposes of this section.

(2) Where a medical practitioner, whose name has ceased to be entered on any list of medical practitioners undertaking to provide general medical services, practises in the area of an Area Health Authority (or of an Executive Council, before its abolition under section 14 of the National Health Service Reorganisation Act 1973) on whose list his name has never been

1973 c. 32.

entered, subsection (1) above does not render unlawful the sale of
the goodwill or any part of the goodwill of his practice in that
area.

(3) Subsection (1) does not prevent the sale of the goodwill or
any part of the goodwill of a medical practice carried on in any
area, being a sale by a medical practitioner whose name has
never been entered on a list of an Area Health Authority (or of
an Executive Council, before its abolition) for that area of medical practitioners undertaking to provide general medical services,
notwithstanding that any part of the goodwill to be sold is
attributable to a practice previously carried on by a person whose
name was entered on such a list.

**55.** Any dispute arising under this Part of this Act or any    Decision of
regulation made under this Part between an Area Health    disputes.
Authority and a person receiving, or claiming that he is entitled
to receive, any services under this Part shall be referred to and
decided by the Secretary of State.

**56.** If the Secretary of State is satisfied, after such inquiry as    Inadequate
he may think fit, as respects any area or part of an area of an    services.
Area Health Authority that the persons whose names are
included in any list prepared under this Part of this Act—

  (a) of medical practitioners undertaking to provide general
      medical services,

  (b) of dental practitioners undertaking to provide general
      dental services,

  (c) of persons undertaking to provide general ophthalmic
      services, or

  (d) of persons undertaking to provide pharmaceutical
      services,

are not such as to secure the adequate provision of the services
in question in that area or part, or that for any other reason
any considerable number of persons in any such area or part are
not receiving satisfactory services under the arrangements in force
under this Part, then—

  (i) he may authorise the Area Health Authority to make
      such other arrangements as he may approve, or may
      himself make other arrangements, and

  (ii) he may dispense with any of the requirements of regula-
       tions made under this Part so far as appears to him
       necessary to meet exceptional circumstances and enable
       such arrangements to be made.

## PART III

### OTHER POWERS OF THE SECRETARY OF STATE AS TO THE HEALTH SERVICE

#### *Control of maximum prices for medical supplies*

Maximum
price of
medical
supplies may
be controlled.

**57.**—(1) The Secretary of State may by order provide for controlling maximum prices to be charged for any medical supplies required for the purposes of this Act.

(2) The Secretary of State may by direction given with respect to any undertaking, or by order made with respect to any class or description of undertakings, being an undertaking or class or description of undertakings concerned with medical supplies required for the purposes of this Act, require persons carrying on the undertaking or undertakings of that class or description—

(a) to keep such books, accounts and records relating to the undertaking as may be prescribed by the direction or, as the case may be, by the order or a notice served under the order ;

(b) to furnish at such times, in such manner and in such form as may be so prescribed such estimates, returns or information relating to the undertaking as may be so prescribed.

(3) The additional provisions set out in Schedule 11 to this Act have effect in relation to this section ; and

" medical supplies " in this section includes surgical, dental and optical materials and equipment ; and

" undertaking " in this section and that Schedule means any public utility undertaking or any undertaking by way of trade or business.

#### *Additional powers as to services and supplies ; and the use of those services and supplies for private patients*

Additional
powers as to
accommoda-
tion and
services.

**58.** The Secretary of State may allow persons to make use (on such terms, including terms as to the payment of charges, as he thinks fit) of any accommodation or services provided under this Act and may provide the accommodation or services in question to an extent greater than that necessary apart from this section if he thinks it expedient so to do in order to allow persons to make use of them.

This section is subject to sections 59, 60 and 62 below.

s. 58 power
in relation
to private
patients.

**59.**—(1) In this section and section 60 below " the section 58 power " means the Secretary of State's power under section 58 above to afford persons (subject to section 62 below) admission or access to accommodation or services as resident or non-resident private patients at health service hospitals.

(2) The Secretary of State shall not in the exercise of his section 58 power afford a person admission or access to accommodation or services at such a hospital as a private patient unless satisfied that the accommodation or services are required for the purposes of investigation, diagnosis or treatment which—

(*a*) is of a specialised nature or involves the use of specialised equipment or skills ; and

(*b*) is not privately available in Great Britain or, if it is so available, either—

(i) is not privately available there at a place which is reasonably accessible to the patient ; or

(ii) is such that it is in the interests of the health service or of the Scottish health service or of both for it to be carried out on that occasion at that hospital.

In this subsection " privately available " means available at a satisfactory standard otherwise than at a health service hospital.

(3) The Secretary of State shall not exercise his section 58 power in such a way as to afford persons admission or access to accommodation or services at health service hospitals otherwise than in accordance with the following arrangements.

Those arrangements are such as in his opinion are best suited for securing that all persons admitted or afforded access to accommodation or services at health service hospitals as resident or non-resident patients for the purposes of investigation, diagnosis or treatment of a specialised nature, or involving the use of specialised equipment or skills, are, so far as is practicable, admitted or afforded such access on the basis of medical priority alone, whether they come as private patients or not.

(4) The Secretary of State shall not exercise his section 58 power in such a way as to allow any particular accommodation or facilities at a health service hospital to be reserved or set aside for regular or repeated use in connection with the treatment of persons as private patients.

This subsection is without prejudice to his power to allow such use in connection with the treatment of any particular person afforded admission or access to that accommodation or those facilities.

**60.**—(1) There shall be made in respect of any exercise of the section 58 power such charges as the Secretary of State may in accordance with subsections (2) and (3) below determine.

Additional provision as to charges under s. 58.

B 4

(2) Without prejudice to the generality of the Secretary of State's section 58 power to make and recover charges for any use which he may under that section allow to be made of any accommodation or services provided under this Act, the Secretary of State may in pursuance of subsection (1) above determine different rates or scales of charges—

(a) for different accommodation or services at different health service hospitals or different classes of such hospitals ;

(b) for different forms or classes of treatment ;

(c) in relation to patients who are, and patients who are not, ordinarily resident in Great Britain ;

(d) generally for different accommodation and for different services and in relation to different circumstances.

(3) The charges determined in pursuance of subsection (1) above—

(a) shall be such as will ensure, so far as is practicable, that no increase in the expenses incurred by the Secretary of State under this Act results from any exercise of the section 58 power ;

(b) shall include such amounts as appear to the Secretary of State proper and reasonable in respect of costs appearing to him to be properly attributable to capital account ; and

(c) in the case of charges for services provided to a private patient at a health service hospital by a whole-time consultant, shall be not less than would be charged by a part-time consultant for providing similar services in similar circumstances to a private patient of his.

(4) Where a health authority receives any sum charged under section 58 for services provided to a private patient by a whole-time consultant—

(a) the authority shall retain that sum and use it for the purposes of research and development in medicine or dentistry, but

(b) if the services in question were provided by a consultant employed by a medical or dental school or university, the authority shall, if so directed by the Secretary of State, pay the sum to that school or university to use for those purposes.

(5) Nothing in this section or in section 59 above prevents the Secretary of State from allowing any medical or dental practitioner employed by a health authority to make use of any accommodation or services provided by virtue of this Act to the extent to which the practitioner would be entitled to make such use under the terms of that employment if those terms were as they were or would have been at the passing of the Health Services Act 1976 c. 83. 1976.

(6) In this section—

"health authority" includes a preserved Board ;

"preserved Board" has the meaning given by section 15(6) of the National Health Service Reorganisation Act 1973 c. 32. 1973 ;

"whole-time consultant" and "part-time consultant" mean respectively a consultant employed whole-time or part-time by a health authority, medical or dental school or university.

**61.**—(1) The Secretary of State may sell or give away, or Additional otherwise dispose of, goods the production or manufacture of powers as to which by him is involved in the provision of services under this disposal and Act. production of goods.

(2) He may, in the case of goods referred to in subsection (1) above which are prescribed for the purposes of this section, produce or manufacture them to an extent greater than that necessitated by the provision of such services in order that they may be supplied to persons other than those to whom they are supplied by way of the provision of such services whether or not the first-mentioned persons are engaged in the provision of other services provided under this Act.

(3) This section is subject to section 62 below.

**62.** The Secretary of State shall exercise the powers conferred Restriction of on him by the provisions of section 25 above (supplies not powers under readily obtainable) and sections 58 and 61 above only if and to ss. 25, 58 and the extent that he is satisfied that anything which he proposes 61. to do or allow under those powers—

(a) will not to a significant extent interfere with the performance by him of any duty imposed on him by this Act to provide accommodation or services of any kind ; and

(b) will not to a significant extent operate to the disadvantage of persons seeking or afforded admission or access to accommodation or services at health service hospitals (whether as resident or non-resident patients) otherwise than as private patients.

*Further provisions as to payments by patients for health service accommodation and services*

Hospital
accommoda-
tion on part
payment.

**63.**—(1) The Secretary of State may authorise the accommodation described in this section to be made available, to such extent
as he may determine, for patients who give an undertaking (or
for whom one is given) to pay such charges for part of the cost
as the Secretary of State may determine, and he may recover
those charges.

The accommodation mentioned above is—

(a) in single rooms or small wards which is not for the time
    being needed by any patient on medical grounds ;

(b) at any health service hospital or group of hospitals, or a
    hospital in which patients are treated under arrange-
    ments made by virtue of section 23 above, or at the
    health service hospitals in a particular area or a hos-
    pital in which patients are so treated.

(2) The Secretary of State may allow such deductions as he
thinks fit from the amount of a charge due by virtue of an undertaking given under this section to be paid for accommodation in
respect of any period during which the accommodation is
temporarily vacated by the person for whom it is made available.

Expenses
payable by
remuneratively
employed
resident
patients.

**64.** The Secretary of State may require any person—

(a) who is a resident patient for whom the Secretary of State
    provides services under this Act ; and

(b) who is absent during the day for the purpose of engaging
    in remunerative employment from the hospital where
    he is a patient,

to pay such part of the cost of his maintenance in the hospital
and any incidental cost as may seem reasonable to the Secretary
of State having regard to the amount of that person's remuneration, and the Secretary of State may recover the amount so
required.

Accommoda-
tion and
services for
private
resident
patients.

**65.**—(1) Subject to section 71 below, if the Secretary of State
is satisfied, in the case of a health service hospital or group of
such hospitals or of the health service hospitals in a particular
area, that it is reasonable to do so—

(a) he may, subject to this section, authorise accommodation
    and services at the hospital or hospitals in question to
    be made available to such extent as he may determine ;
    and

(b) that accommodation and those services shall be avail-
    able for resident patients who give an undertaking (or
    for whom one is given) to pay such charges as he may

determine in accordance with the following provisions of this section, and the Secretary of State may recover those charges.

(2) The Secretary of State may allow accommodation and services to which an authorisation under subsection (1) above relates to be made available in connection with treatment, in pursuance of arrangements made by a medical practitioner or dental practitioner serving (whether in an honorary or paid capacity) on the staff of a health service hospital, of private patients of that practitioner as resident patients.

(3) The Secretary of State, for the purpose of determining charges to be paid under subsection (1) above—

    (a) may classify the health service hospitals, and may, in the case of each class, determine in respect of each period of 12 months beginning with 1st April first falling after the date on which the determination is made the charges to be paid under that subsection in respect of accommodation and services provided during that period at a hospital falling within that class;

    (b) in determining such charges in respect of a period the Secretary of State shall have regard, so far as is reasonably practicable, to the total cost (exclusive of costs appearing to him to be properly attributable to capital account) which, by reference to facts known to him at the time of the determination, it is estimated will be incurred during that period in the provision for resident patients of services at hospitals falling within that class; and

    (c) may include in any such charges, in such cases as appear to him fit, such amounts as appear to him proper and reasonable to be included by way of contribution to expenditure appearing to him to be properly attributable to capital account.

(4) The Secretary of State may under subsection (3) above determine different charges for different accommodation and for different services and in relation to different circumstances.

(5) The Secretary of State may allow such deduction as he thinks proper from the amount of a charge due by virtue of an undertaking given under this section by or in respect of any patient—

    (a) in respect of treatment given to the patient under subsection (2) above ; and

    (b) in respect of any period during which the accommodation to which the undertaking relates is temporarily vacated by the patient.

PART III

(6) Nothing in this section prevents accommodation from being made available for a patient other than one mentioned in subsection (1) above if the use of that accommodation is needed more urgently for him on medical grounds than for a patient so mentioned, and no other suitable accommodation is available.

Accommodation and services for private non-resident patients.

**66.**—(1) If the Secretary of State is satisfied, in the case of a health service hospital or group of such hospitals or of the health service hospitals in a particular area, that it is reasonable to do so—

(a) he may, subject to section 71 below, authorise accommodation and services at the hospital or hospitals in question to be made available to such extent as he may determine, and

(b) that accommodation and those services shall be available in connection with treatment, in pursuance of arrangements made by a medical practitioner or dental practitioner serving (whether in an honorary or paid capacity) on the staff of any such hospital, of private patients of that practitioner otherwise than as resident patients.

Those patients shall be patients who give an undertaking (or for whom one is given) to pay, in respect of the accommodation and services, such charges as the Secretary of State may determine, and he may recover those charges.

(2) The Secretary of State may under subsection (1) above determine different charges for different accommodation and for different services, and in relation to different circumstances.

(3) No accommodation and no services shall be so made available under subsection (1) above as to prejudice persons availing themselves of services at a hospital otherwise than as private patients.

*Withdrawal of health service pay beds and services*
*from private patients*

Withdrawal of facilities available for private patients.

**67.**—(1) Sections 68 to 71 below have effect for the purpose of—

(a) securing the separation of the facilities available in England and Wales for the prevention, diagnosis and treatment of illness under private arrangements from the facilities available for those purposes at premises vested in the Secretary of State ; and

(b) to that end securing the progressive withdrawal of accommodation and services at health service hospitals from use in connection with the treatment of persons at such hospitals as resident or non-resident private patients.

(2) Nothing in this Part of this Act prejudices the opera- PART III
tion of paragraph 10(4) of Schedule 5 to this Act (by virtue of
which regulations governing the terms of employment of officers
employed by an authority within the meaning of sub-paragraph
(4) of that paragraph must not contain a requirement that all
consultants so employed shall be so employed whole-time).

**68.**—(1) It continues to be the duty of the Health Services Revocation of
Board to submit to the Secretary of State from time to time in authorisations
accordance with this section proposals for the progressive revo- under s. 65 or
cation of— s. 66.

> (a) the authorisations under section 65(1) above or those
> granted by virtue of section 71(3) below, and
>
> (b) the authorisations under section 66(1) above or those
> granted by virtue of section 71(3) below,

and it shall be the Secretary of State's duty to give effect to all
proposals so submitted.

(2) The Health Services Board shall in the 6 months beginning with the date on which its first proposals were submitted
under section 4(2) of the Health Services Act 1976, and in each 1976 c. 83.
successive period of 6 months thereafter, submit further proposals
under this section or, if in all the circumstances it decides that
the submission of further proposals in any particular period of
6 months is unnecessary, shall instead prepare and submit to
the Secretary of State a report explaining the Board's reasons
for that decision.

(3) In formulating proposals under this section the Board
shall—

> (a) have regard to the principles set out in section 70
> below ; and
>
> (b) consider any representations made to the Board by—
>
>> (i) the Secretary of State ;
>>
>> (ii) any body which is representative of medical
>> practitioners or dental practitioners or of persons
>> employed in the health service or concerned with the
>> interests of patients at health service hospitals ;
>>
>> (iii) any other person having a substantial interest
>> in the proposals.

In deciding what advice to give the Board in connection
with the formulation of any such proposals the Board's Welsh
Committee shall likewise have regard to the principles set out
in section 70 and shall consider any representations made to the
Committee by any of the persons or bodies above mentioned.

(4) Each set of proposals under this section shall specify—

    (*a*) the accommodation and services authorisation of which under section 65(1) or section 66(1) should be revoked, and

    (*b*) the date before which the necessary revocations should take effect,

and may specify different dates for different accommodation or services so specified.

Further
provisions as
to revocation
of s. 66
authorisations.
    **69.**—(1) Without prejudice to subsection (3) of section 68 above, the Health Services Board, in formulating proposals under that section for the revocation of authorisations given under section 66(1) above in respect of accommodation or services at any particular health service hospital or hospitals, and the Welsh Committee in deciding what advice to give the Board in connection with the formulation of any such proposals—

    (*a*) shall have regard to the purposes and specialties for which the accommodation or services in question are available for use in connection with the treatment of non-resident private patients, and

    (*b*) shall apply the principles set out in section 70 below separately in respect of different purposes and specialties,

and the Board may formulate separate proposals in respect of different purposes or specialties accordingly.

    (2) As regards the revocation of authorisations under section 66(1), any proposals under section 68 relating to—

    (*a*) accommodation available to consultants for the purpose of affording consultations to their private patients, or

    (*b*) accommodation and services available for the following specialties, namely, radiotherapy, diagnostic pathology and diagnostic radiology (including scanning, ultrasonics and methods involving the use of radio-isotopes),

shall be formulated by the Board as separate proposals ; and (without prejudice to section 68(1) to (3) above and subsection (1) above) the Board's first proposals under section 4(2) of the Health Services Act 1976 (submitted within 6 months of the passing of that Act or such longer period as the Secretary of State may allow) shall include separate proposals relating to accommodation available to consultants as mentioned in paragraph (*a*) above.

1976 c. 83.

    (3) Without prejudice to section 68 and the preceding provisions of this section, the Health Services Board shall, as regards the revocation of authorisations under section 66(1), submit separate proposals under section 68 relating to—

    (*a*) accommodation and services available for the specialties other than radiotherapy mentioned in subsection (2)(*b*) above, and

(*b*) other accommodation and services available for
diagnostic purposes,
and shall do so not later than the end of the 12 months following
the initial period defined by the Health Services Act 1976 (that 1976 c. 83.
is the period of 6 months beginning with the date on which that
Act was passed), or, if a period longer than the initial period
has been allowed under that Act for the submission of the Board's
first proposals under this section, the 12 months following that
longer period.

**70.** The principles referred to in sections 68 and 69 above Principles as
are— to proposals
under s. 68 or
(*a*) that accommodation or services at any particular health s. 69.
service hospital or hospitals should remain authorised
under section 65(1) or section 66(1) above for use in
connection with the treatment of resident or non-
resident private patients only while there is a reasonable
demand for accommodation and facilities for the
private practice of medicine and dentistry in the area
or areas served by the hospital or hospitals in
question ;

(*b*) that the authorisation of any such accommodation or
services under those provisions for use in that
connection should be revoked only if sufficient
accommodation and facilities for the private practice
of medicine and dentistry are otherwise reasonably
available (whether privately or at health service
hospitals) to meet the reasonable demand for them
in the area or areas served by the hospital or hospitals
in question ;

(*c*) that the continued authorisation of any such accommodation or services under those provisions for use
in that connection should depend on there having been
or being taken all reasonable steps to provide, otherwise
than at health service hospitals, sufficient reasonable
accommodation and facilities for the private practice
of medicine and dentistry to meet the reasonable
demand for them in the area or areas served by the
hospital or hospitals in question ;

(*d*) that failure, in the circumstances mentioned in
paragraph (*c*) above, to take all reasonable steps that
could be taken to provide as mentioned in that
paragraph would itself be grounds for the Health
Services Board, after giving due warning to persons
likely to be affected thereby of the likely consequences
of such failure, to propose the revocation of the
authorisations under those provisions relating to
accommodation or services at the hospital or hospitals
in question.

**71.**—(1) No authorisation—

   (*a*) under section 65(1) or section 66(1) above shall be
        granted, except by virtue of subsection (2) or subsection
        (4) below ; and

   (*b*) shall be, other than one granted on a temporary basis
        as mentioned in subsection (4), to any extent revoked
        otherwise than in accordance with proposals submitted
        to the Secretary of State by the Health Services Board
        under section 68 above.

(2) The Health Services Board may submit to the Secretary of
State proposals for securing that in any case where one or
more beds authorised under section 65(1) cease to be available
to resident private patients, or any accommodation or services
authorised under section 66(1) cease to be available to non-
resident private patients, in consequence of the permanent closure
of any health service hospital accommodation in England or
Wales independently of any proposals submitted by the Board
under section 68, the total number of effective beds, or the total
amount of effective accommodation or services, as the case may
be, so authorised in England or Wales is not thereby reduced
below what it would be if—

   (*a*) the closed accommodation had remained in use, but

   (*b*) effect had been given by the Secretary of State to all
        proposals under section 68 received by him before the
        submission of the proposals in question under this
        subsection.

(3) It shall be the Secretary of State's duty to grant such
authorisations under section 65(1) or section 66(1), as the case
may be, as are needed to give effect to any proposals submitted
to him under subsection (2) above.

(4) Where any health service hospital accommodation in England or Wales is temporarily closed (whether at the instance of
the Secretary of State or not) for physical or other reasons outside his control, the Secretary of State shall, without the need for
any proposals by the Board, grant on a temporary basis such
authorisations under section 65(1) or section 66(1) as he would
have been able to grant by virtue of subsections (2) and (3)
above if—

   (*a*) the closure had been permanent ; and

   (*b*) the Board had submitted to him any proposals which it
        could in that case have submitted to him under sub-
        section (2).

(5) Subject to the restrictions imposed by this section, section
65 or, as the case may be, section 66 continue to have effect in
relation to any accommodation or services to which an authorisation under section 65(1) or section 66(1) relates.

*Use by practitioners of health service facilities for private practice*

**72.**—(1) A person to whom this section applies who wishes to use any relevant health service accommodation or facilities for the purpose of providing medical, dental, pharmaceutical, ophthalmic or chiropody services to non-resident private patients may apply in writing to the Secretary of State for permission under this section.

(2) Any application for permission under this section must specify—

   (a) which of the relevant health service accommodation or facilities the applicant wishes to use for the purpose of providing services to such patients ; and

   (b) which of the kinds of services mentioned in subsection (1) above he wishes the permission to cover.

(3) On receiving an application under this section the Secretary of State—

   (a) shall consider whether anything for which permission is sought would interfere with the giving of full and proper attention to persons seeking or afforded access otherwise than as private patients to any services provided under this Act ; and

   (b) shall grant the permission applied for unless in his opinion anything for which permission is sought would so interfere.

(4) Any grant of permssion under this section shall be on such terms (including terms as to the payment of charges for the use of the relevant health service accommodation or facilities pursuant to the permission) as the Secretary of State may from time to time determine.

(5) The persons to whom this section applies are—

   (a) persons of any of the following descriptions who provide services under Part II of this Act, namely, medical practitioners, dental practitioners, registered pharmacists, and ophthalmic or dispensing opticians ; and

   (b) other persons who provide pharmaceutical or ophthalmic services under Part II ; and

   (c) chiropodists who provide services under this Act at premises where services are provided under Part II.

(6) In this section—

   (a) " relevant health service accommodation or facilities ", in relation to a person to whom this section applies, means any accommodation or facilities available at premises provided by the Secretary of State by virtue of this Act, being accommodation or facilities which that person is for the time being authorised to use for purposes of Part II ; or

(b) in the case of a person to whom this section applies by virtue of paragraph (c) of subsection (5) above, accommodation or facilities which that person is for the time being authorised to use for purposes of this Act at premises where services are provided under Part II.

*Information and reports*

Information for Health Services Board.

**73.** It is the Secretary of State's duty to furnish the Health Services Board with such information as it may reasonably require for the proper discharge of its functions under sections 68 to 71 above.

Publication of matters under ss. 68 and 71.

**74.** The Secretary of State shall cause every set of proposals submitted to him under sections 68 and 71 above, and every report submitted to him under section 68(2), to be published as soon as practicable after its submission, and shall lay a copy of every such set of proposals or report before each House of Parliament.

Reports on extent of facilities for private patients.

**75.**—(1) There shall be prepared by the Secretary of State on the matters mentioned in subsection (2) below an annual report relating to England and one relating to Wales, and he shall lay a copy of every report under this section before each House of Parliament.

(2) The matters referred to under subsection (1) above are—

(a) the accommodation and services at health service hospitals which in the period covered by the report were available for use in connection with the treatment of private patients by virtue of authorisations under sections 65(1) and 66(1) above ;

(b) the extent to which " the section 58 power " (as defined in section 59(1) above) was exercised in that period ;

(c) the extent to which the powers to which section 62 above applies were exercised in that period otherwise than by way of affording persons admission or access to accommodation or services at health service hospitals as resident or non-resident private patients ; and

(d) the extent to which progress has been made in implementing the common waiting-lists referred to in section 6 of the Health Services Act 1976, and in section 76 below.

1976 c. 83.

**76.**—(1) The reference in paragraph (*d*) of section 75(2) above PART III to common waiting-lists is to the recommendations made to the " Common Secretary of State by the Health Services Board under section waiting-lists ". 6(1) of the Health Services Act 1976. 1976 c. 83.

(2) Those recommendations—

  (*a*) related to arrangements for affording persons admission or access as resident patients (authorised under section 65 above) or non-resident patients (authorised under section 66 above) to accommodation and services ; and

  (*b*) were in the Board's opinion the ones best suited for securing that all persons admitted or afforded access to accommodation or services at health service hospitals as resident or non-resident patients are, so far as practicable, admitted or afforded access thereto on the basis of medical priority alone, whether coming as private patients or not.

### Regulations as to certain charges

**77.**—(1) Regulations may provide for the making and recovery Charges in such manner as may be prescribed of such charges as may be for drugs, prescribed in respect of— medicines or appliances, or

  (*a*) the supply under this Act (otherwise than under Part II) pharmaceutical of drugs, medicines or appliances (including the re- services. placement and repair of those appliances),

  (*b*) such of the pharmaceutical services referred to in Part II as may be prescribed,

and paragraphs (*a*) and (*b*) of this subsection may include the supply of substances and appliances mentioned in paragraph (*b*) of section 5(1) above.

(2) Regulations under subsection (1) above may provide for the grant, on payment of such sums as may be prescribed by those regulations, of certificates conferring on the persons to whom the certificates are granted exemption from charges otherwise exigible under the regulations in respect of drugs, medicines and appliances supplied during such period as may be prescribed, and different sums may be so prescribed in relation to different periods.

(3) The additional provisions of paragraphs 1 and 4 of Schedule 12 to this Act have effect in relation to this section.

**78.**—(1) Regulations may provide for the making and recovery Charges in such manner as may be prescribed of charges of such for dental amounts as are mentioned in sub-paragraph (1) of paragraph 2 or optical of Schedule 12 to this Act, in respect of the supply under the appliances. Act of such dental or optical appliances as are mentioned in that sub-paragraph.

PART III    (2) If the Secretary of State, after consultation with the university associated with any hospital providing facilities for clinical dental teaching, is satisfied that it is expedient in the interests of dental training or education that the charges imposed by subsection (1) above should be remitted in the case of dental services provided at that hospital, either generally or subject to limitations or conditions, he may by order provide for that purpose.

Any order made under this subsection may be revoked or varied by a subsequent order made by the Secretary of State after such consultation as is mentioned above.

(3) The additional provisions of paragraphs 2 and 5 of Schedule 12 have effect in relation to this section.

Charges for dental treatment.    **79.**—(1) A charge of the amount authorised by this section may be made and recovered, in such manner as may be prescribed, in respect of any services provided as part of the general dental services under Part II of this Act, not being—

>    (*a*) the supply or replacement of appliances mentioned in paragraph 2(1) of Schedule 12 to this Act;
>    (*b*) the repair of appliances other than prescribed appliances;
>    (*c*) the arrest of bleeding; or
>    (*d*) the clinical examination of a patient and any report on that examination.

The additional provisions of paragraphs 3 and 5 of Schedule 12 have effect in relation to this subsection.

(2) Regulations may provide that, in the case of such special dental treatment as may be prescribed, being treatment provided as part of the general dental services, such charges as may be prescribed may be made and recovered by the person providing the services.

Charges for designated facilities.    **80.** Regulations may provide for the making and recovery of charges in respect of facilities designated by the regulations as facilities provided in pursuance of paragraph (*d*) or paragraph (*e*) of section 3(1) above.

Charges for more expensive supplies.    **81.** Regulations may provide for the making and recovery of such charges as may be prescribed—

>    (*a*) by the Secretary of State in respect of the supply by him of any appliance or vehicle which is, at the request of the person supplied, of a more expensive type than the prescribed type, or in respect of the replacement or repair of any such appliance, or the replacement of any such vehicle, or the taking of any such action in

relation to the vehicle as is mentioned in paragraph 1 of Schedule 2 to this Act ;

(*b*) by persons providing general dental services or general ophthalmic services in respect of the supply, as part of those services, of any dental or optical appliance which is, at the request of the person supplied, of a more expensive type than the prescribed type or in respect of the replacement or repair of any such appliance.

**82.** Regulations may provide for the making and recovery of such charges as may be prescribed— Charges for repairs and replacements in certain cases.

(*a*) by the Secretary of State in respect of the replacement or repair of any appliance or vehicle supplied by him,

or

(*b*) by persons providing general dental services or general ophthalmic services in respect of the replacement or repair of any dental or optical appliance supplied as part of those services,

if it is determined in the prescribed manner that the replacement or repair is necessitated by an act or omission of the person supplied or (if the act or omission occurred when the person supplied was under 16 years of age) of the person supplied or of the person having charge of him when the act or omission occurred.

**83.** Regulations made— Sums otherwise payable to those providing services.

(*a*) under sections 77 to 79 and under sections 81 and 82 above providing for the making and recovery of charges in respect of any services, may provide for the reduction of the sums which would otherwise be payable by a Regional Health Authority, an Area Health Authority or a Family Practitioner Committee to the persons by whom those services are provided by the amount of the charges authorised by the regulations in respect of those services ;

(*b*) for the purposes of section 78(1) in relation to appliances provided as part of the general dental services or the general ophthalmic services under Part II of this Act, may provide for the reduction of the sums which would otherwise be payable by an Area Health Authority or a Family Practitioner Committee to the persons by whom those services are provided by the amount of the charges authorised by section 78(1) in respect of those appliances.

*Inquiries, and default and emergency powers*

**84.**—(1) The Secretary of State may cause an inquiry to be held in any case where he deems it advisable to do so in connection with any matter arising under this Act.

(2) For the purpose of any such inquiry (but subject to subsection (3) below) the person appointed to hold the inquiry—

(a) may by summons require any person to attend, at a time and place stated in the summons, to give evidence or to produce any documents in his custody or under his control which relate to any matter in question at the inquiry ; and

(b) may take evidence on oath, and for that purpose administer oaths, or may, instead of administering an oath, require the person examined to make a solemn affirmation.

(3) Nothing in this section—

(a) requires a person, in obedience to a summons under the section, to attend to give evidence or to produce any documents unless the necessary expenses of his attendance are paid or tendered to him ; or

(b) empowers the person holding the inquiry to require the production of the title, or of any instrument relating to the title, of any land not being the property of a local authority.

(4) Any person who refuses or deliberately fails to attend in obedience to a summons under this section, or to give evidence, or who deliberately alters, suppresses, conceals, destroys, or refuses to produce any book or other document which he is required or is liable to be required to produce for the purposes of this section, shall be liable on summary conviction to a fine not exceeding £100 or to imprisonment for a term not exceeding 6 months, or to both.

(5) Where the Secretary of State causes an inquiry to be held under this section—

(a) the costs incurred by him in relation to the inquiry (including such reasonable sum not exceeding £30 a day as he may determine for the services of any officer engaged in the inquiry) shall be paid by such local authority or party to the inquiry as he may direct, and

(b) he may cause the amount of the costs so incurred to be certified, and any amount so certified and directed to be paid by any authority or person shall be recoverable from that authority or person by the Secretary of State summarily as a civil debt.

No local authority shall be ordered to pay costs under this subsection in the case of any inquiry unless it is a party to that inquiry.

(6) Where the Secretary of State causes an inquiry to be held under this section he may make orders—

(a) as to the costs of the parties at the inquiry, and

(b) as to the parties by whom the costs are to be paid,

and every such order may be made a rule of the High Court on the application of any party named in the order.

**85.**—(1) Where the Secretary of State is of opinion, on complaint or otherwise, that— Default powers.

(a) any Regional Health Authority ;

(b) any Area Health Authority ;

(c) any special health authority ;

(d) any Family Practitioner Committee ;

(e) any local social services authority ;

(f) the Medical Practices Committee ; or

(g) the Dental Estimates Board ;

have failed to carry out any functions conferred or imposed on them by or under this Act, or have in carrying out those functions failed to comply with any regulations or directions relating to those functions, he may after such inquiry as he may think fit make an order declaring them to be in default.

(2) Except where the body in default is a local social services authority, the members of the body shall forthwith vacate their office, and the order—

(a) shall provide for the appointment, in accordance with the provisions of this Act, of new members of the body ; and

(b) may contain such provisions as seem to the Secretary of State expedient for authorising any person to act in the place of the body in question pending the appointment of new members.

(3) If the body in default is a local social services authority—

(a) the order shall direct them, for the purpose of remedying the default, to discharge such of their functions, in such manner and within such time or times, as may be specified in the order ; and

(b) if the authority fail to comply with any direction given under this subsection within the time so limited, the Secretary of State, instead of enforcing the order by mandamus or otherwise, may make an order transferring to himself such of the functions of the authority as he thinks fit.

(4) Any expenses certified by the Secretary of State to have been incurred by him in discharging functions transferred to him under this section from a local social services authority shall on demand be paid to him by that authority and shall be recoverable by him from them as a debt due to the Crown ; and

    (a) the authority or (in the case of a joint board) any constituent local authority thereof shall have the like power of raising the money required as they have of raising money for paying expenses incurred directly by them ; and

    (b) the payment of any such expenses so incurred by the Secretary of State shall, to such extent as he may sanction, be a purpose for which the authority may borrow money in accordance with the statutory provisions relating to borrowing by that authority.

(5) An order made under this section may contain such supplementary and incidental provisions as appear to the Secretary of State to be necessary or expedient, including—

    (a) provision for the transfer to the Secretary of State of property and liabilities of the body in default ; and

    (b) where any such order is varied or revoked by a subsequent order, provision in the revoking order or a subsequent order for the transfer to the body in default of any property or liabilities acquired or incurred by the Secretary of State in discharging any of the functions transferred to him.

Emergency powers.

**86.** If the Secretary of State—

    (a) considers that by reason of an emergency it is necessary, in order to ensure that a service falling to be provided in pursuance of this Act is provided, to direct that during the period specified by the directions a function conferred on any body or person by virtue of this Act shall to the exclusion of or concurrently with that body or person be performed by another body or person, then

    (b) he may give directions accordingly and it shall be the duty of the bodies or persons in question to comply with the directions.

The powers conferred on the Secretary of State by this section are in addition to any other powers exercisable by him.

## PART IV

### PROPERTY AND FINANCE

#### *Land and other Property*

87.—(1) The Secretary of State may acquire—

Acquisition,
use and
maintenance
of property.

   (*a*) any land, either by agreement or compulsorily,

   (*b*) any other property,

required by him for the purposes of this Act ; and (without prejudice to the generality of paragraph (*a*) above) land may be so
acquired to provide residential accommodation for persons
employed for any of those purposes.

(2) The Secretary of State may use for the purposes of any of
the functions conferred on him by this Act any property belonging to him by virtue of this Act, and he has power to
maintain all such property.

(3) A local social services authority may be authorised to purchase land compulsorily for the purposes of this Act by means of
an order made by the authority and confirmed by the Secretary
of State.

(4) The Acquisition of Land (Authorisation Procedure) Act 1946 c. 49.
1946 shall apply to the compulsory purchase of land by the
Secretary of State under this section, and accordingly shall have
effect—

   (*a*) as if section 1(1) of that Act (which refers to the
compulsory purchase of land by local authorities under
public general Acts in force immediately before the
commencement of that Act and by the Minister of
Transport under certain enactments) included a reference to any compulsory purchase of land by the Secretary of State under this section ; and

   (*b*) as if this section had been in force immediately before
the commencement of that Act.

(5) Section 120(3) of the Local Government Act 1972 (which 1972 c. 70.
relates to the application of Part I of the Compulsory Purchase 1965 c. 56.
Act 1965 where a council are authorised to acquire land by
agreement) applies to the acquisition of land by the Secretary of
State under this section in like manner as it applies to such
acquisition by a council under that section.

(6) Section 128 of the Town and Country Planning Act 1971 1971 c. 78.
(use and development of consecrated land and burial grounds)
applies to consecrated land and land comprised in a burial
ground within the meaning of that section which—

   (*a*) the Secretary of State holds for any of the purposes of
the health service, and

PART IV

(b) has not been acquired by him as mentioned in subsection (1) of that section,

as if that land had been so acquired for those purposes.

Transferred
property free
of trusts.
1946 c. 81.

**88.**—(1) All property vested in the Secretary of State in consequence of the transfer of that property under section 6 of the National Health Service Act 1946 (transfer of hospitals) so vests free of any trust existing immediately before that transfer.

(2) The Secretary of State may use any such property for the purpose of any of his functions under this Act, but he shall so far as practicable secure that the objects for which any such property was used immediately before that transfer are not prejudiced by section 6 of that Act of 1946.

Power of
voluntary
organisations
to transfer
property.

**89.** Notwithstanding anything contained—

(a) in the constitution or rules of any voluntary organisation formed for the purpose of providing a service of nurses for attendance on the sick in their own homes, or of midwives, or

(b) in any trust deed or other instrument relating to such organisation or service,

any property vested in the organisation or held by any persons on trust for the organisation or service or for any specific purposes connected with the organisation or service may be transferred to the Secretary of State, on such terms as may be agreed between him and the organisation or trustees, with a view to the property being used or held by him for purposes similar to the purposes for which it was previously used or held.

*Trusts*

Gifts
on trust.

**90.** A health authority has power to accept, hold and administer any property on trust for all or any purposes relating to the health service.

Private trusts
for hospitals.

**91.**—(1) Where—

(a) the terms of a trust instrument authorise or require the trustees, whether immediately or in the future, to apply any part of the capital or income of the trust property for the purposes of any health service hospital, then

(b) the trust instrument shall be construed as authorising or (as the case may be) requiring the trustees to apply the trust property to the like extent, and at the like times, for the purpose of making payments, whether of capital or income, to the appropriate hospital authority.

(2) Any sum so paid to the appropriate hospital authority shall, so far as practicable, be applied by them for the purpose specified in the trust instrument.

(3) In this section "the appropriate hospital authority" means—

    (a) where special trustees are appointed for the hospital, those trustees ;

    (b) in any other case, the Area Health Authority exercising functions on behalf of the Secretary of State in respect of the hospital.

(4) Nothing in this section applies to a trust for a special hospital, or to property transferred under section 24 of the National Health Service Reorganisation Act 1973. 1973 c. 32.

**92.**—(1) The Secretary of State may, having regard to any change or proposed change in the arrangements for the adminis- Further tration of a hospital or in the area or functions of any health authority, by order provide for the transfer of any trust property from any health authority or special trustees to any other health authority or special trustees. Further transfers of trust property.

(2) If it appears to the Secretary of State at any time that all the functions of any special trustees should be discharged by one or more health authorities then, whether or not there has been any such change as is mentioned in subsection (1) above, he may by order provide for the transfer of all trust property from the special trustees to the health authority, or, in such proportions as he may specify in the order, to those health authorities.

(3) Before so acting the Secretary of State shall consult the health authorities and special trustees concerned.

(4) Where by an order under this section, property is transferred to two or more authorities, it shall be apportioned by them in such proportions as they may agree or as may in default of agreement be determined by the Secretary of State, and the order may provide for the way in which the property is to be apportioned.

(5) Where property is so apportioned, the Secretary of State may by order make any consequential amendments of the trust instrument relating to the property.

PART IV

Trust property
previously held
for general
hospital
purposes.
1973 c. 32.

1946 c. 81.

**93.**—(1) This section applies—

(*a*) to property transferred under section 23 of the National
Health Service Reorganisation Act 1973 (winding-up
of hospital endowments funds), and

(*b*) to property transferred under section 24 of that Act
(transfer of trust property from abolished authorities)
which immediately before the day appointed for the
purposes of that section was, in accordance with any
provision contained in or made under section 7 of the
National Health Service Act 1946, applicable for
purposes relating to hospital services or relating to
some form of research,

and this section continues to apply to the property after any
further transfer under section 92 above.

(2) The person holding the property after the transfer or last
transfer shall secure, so far as is reasonably practicable, that the
objects of any original endowment and the observance of any
conditions attached to that endowment, including in particular
conditions intended to preserve the memory of any person or
class of persons, are not prejudiced by this Part of this Act, or
Part II of that Act of 1973.

In this subsection " original endowment " means a hospital
endowment which was transferred under section 7 of that Act
of 1946 and from which the property in question is derived.

(3) Subject to subsection (2) above, the property shall be held
on trust for such purposes relating to hospital services (including
research), or to any other part of the health service associated
with any hospital, as the person holding the property thinks fit.

(4) Where the person holding the property is a body of special
trustees, the power conferred by subsection (3) above shall be
exercised as respects the hospitals for which they are appointed.

**94.**—(1) Any discretion given by a trust instrument to the
trustees of property transferred under—

(*a*) section 24 of the National Health Service Reorganisation Act 1973 (transfer of trust property from abolished
authorities),

(*b*) section 25 of that Act (transfer of trust property held
for health services by local health authorities),

(*c*) section 92 above,

shall be exercisable by the person to whom the property is so
transferred and, subject to section 93 above and the following
provisions of this section, the transfer shall not affect the trusts
on which the property is held.

(2) Where—

    (a) property has been transferred under section 24 of that Act of 1973, and

    (b) any discretion is given by a trust instrument to the trustees to apply the property, or income arising from the property, to such hospital services (including research) as the trustees think fit without any restriction on the kinds of hospital services and without any restriction to one or more specified hospitals,

the discretion shall be enlarged so as to allow the application of the property or (as the case may be) of the income arising from the property, to such extent as the trustees think fit, for any other part of the health service associated with any hospital.

(3) Subsection (2) above shall apply on any subsequent transfer of the property under section 92 above.

**95.**—(1) The bodies of trustees (in this Act referred to as special trustees) appointed by the Secretary of State under section 29 of the National Health Service Reorganisation Act 1973 and this section shall (subject to section 92 above) hold and administer the property transferred to them under that Act of 1973. Special trustees for a university or teaching hospital.<br>1973 c. 32.

The special trustees so appointed are bodies of trustees appointed for the hospital or hospitals which, immediately before the day appointed for the purposes of section 29 of that Act of 1973, were controlled and managed by a University Hospital Management Committee or a Board of Governors, but excluding—

    (a) a body on whose request an order was made under section 24(2) of that Act of 1973 ;

    (b) a preserved Board within the meaning of section 15(6) of that Act of 1973.

(2) Special trustees have power to accept, hold and administer any property on trust for all or any purposes relating to hospital services (including research), or to any other part of the health service associated with hospitals, being a trust which is wholly or mainly for hospitals for which the special trustees are appointed.

(3) The number of trustees for any hospital or hospitals shall be such as the Secretary of State may from time to time determine after consultation with such persons as he considers appropriate.

(4) The term of office of any special trustee shall be fixed by the Secretary of State but a special trustee may be removed by the Secretary of State at any time during the special trustee's term of office.

PART IV
Trusts: supple-
mentary
provisions.

1960 c. 58.

1895 c. 16.

**96.**—(1) Any provision in sections 90 to 95 above for the transfer of any property includes provision for the transfer of any rights and liabilities arising from that property.

(2) Nothing in those sections shall affect any power of Her Majesty, the court (as defined in the Charities Act 1960) or any other person to alter the trusts of any charity.

(3) Nothing in section 12 of the Finance Act 1895 (which requires certain Acts and certain instruments relating to the vesting of property by virtue of an Act to be stamped as conveyances on sale) applies to sections 90 to 95 above or to an order made in pursuance of any of those sections ; and stamp duty shall not be payable on such an order.

### Finance and Accounts

Expenses of
health
authorities.

**97.**—(1) It is the Secretary of State's duty to pay—

(a) to each Area Health Authority in Wales and each Regional Health Authority the sums needed to defray such expenditure of the Authority as the Secretary of State approves in the prescribed manner ;

(b) to each Family Practitioner Committee sums equal to the expenses which the Secretary of State determines are incurred by the Committee for the purpose of performing the functions conferred on the Committee by virtue of this Act ; and

(c) to each special health authority sums equal to such of the expenses of the authority as are not defrayed by payments made to the authority in pursuance of subsection (3) below.

(2) It is the duty of each Regional Health Authority to pay to each Area Health Authority of which the area is included in the region of the Regional Health Authority the sums needed to defray such expenses of the Area Health Authority as the Regional Health Authority approves in the prescribed manner.

(3) Where an order establishing a special health authority provides for any expenses of the authority to be defrayed by a Regional or Area Health Authority or by two or more such Authorities in portions determined by or in accordance with the order, it is the duty of each Authority in question to pay to the special health authority sums equal to, or to the appropriate portion of, those expenses.

(4) Sums falling to be paid under this section shall be payable subject to compliance with such conditions as to records, certificates or otherwise as the Secretary of State may determine.

**98.**—(1) Accounts, in such form as the Secretary of State may    PART IV
with the approval of the Treasury direct, shall be kept by—    Accounts and
audit.

    (a) every Regional Health Authority ;

    (b) every Area Health Authority ;

    (c) every special health authority ;

    (d) all special trustees appointed in pursuance of section
       29(1) of the National Health Service Reorganisation 1973 c. 32.
       Act 1973 and section 95(1) above ;

    (e) the Dental Estimates Board.

Those accounts shall be audited by auditors appointed by the
Secretary of State, and the Comptroller and Auditor General
may examine all such accounts and any records relating to them,
and any report of the auditor on them.

(2) Every such body shall prepare and transmit to the Secretary of State in respect of each financial year annual accounts
in such form as the Secretary of State may with the approval of
the Treasury direct.

The accounts prepared and transmitted by an Area Health
Authority in pursuance of this subsection shall include annual
accounts of the Family Practitioner Committees established by
the Authority and of any Community Health Council of which
the district includes any part of the Authority's area.

(3) The Secretary of State may by regulations provide
generally with respect to the audit under subsection (1) above
of accounts of bodies to which that subsection applies ; and in
particular for conferring on the auditor of any of those
accounts—

    (a) such rights of access to, and production of, books,
       accounts, vouchers or other documents as may be
       specified in the regulations ; and

    (b) such right, in such conditions as may be so specified,
       to require from any member or officer, or former
       member or officer, of any such body, such information
       relating to the affairs of the body as the Secretary of
       State may think necessary for the proper performance
       of the auditor's duty under this section.

(4) The Secretary of State shall prepare in respect of each
financial year—

    (a) in such form as the Treasury may direct, summarised
       accounts of those Authorities, special authorities and
       special trustees :

(*b*) in such form and containing such information as the Treasury may direct, a statement of the accounts of the Dental Estimates Board ;

and shall transmit them on or before 30th November in each year to the Comptroller and Auditor General, who shall examine and certify them, and lay copies of them together with his report on them before both Houses of Parliament.

Regulation of financial arrangements.

**99.**—(1) The Secretary of State may by regulations provide, in the case of all or any of the following bodies—

(*a*) Regional Health Authorities,

(*b*) Area Health Authorities,

(*c*) special health authorities,

(*d*) Family Practitioner Committees,

(*e*) Community Health Councils, and

(*f*) the Dental Estimates Board,

for restricting the making of payments by or on behalf of the body otherwise than on such authorisation and subject to such conditions as may be specified in the regulations.

(2) Such provision may be made subject to such exceptions as may be so specified, and those regulations may contain such other provisions as to the making and carrying out by all or any of those bodies of such arrangements with respect to financial matters as the Secretary of State thinks necessary for the purpose of securing that the affairs of such bodies are conducted, so far as reasonably practicable, in such manner as to prevent financial loss and to ensure and maintain efficiency.

(3) The Secretary of State may give directions to any of those bodies as to any matter with respect to which those regulations may be made ; and those directions may be specific in character and shall be—

(*a*) such as appear to him requisite to secure that the affairs of the body are conducted in such a manner as is mentioned in subsection (2) above,

(*b*) without prejudice to the operation of any such regulations,

and shall be complied with by the body to whom they are given.

Other Payments.

**100.**—(1) There shall be paid out of moneys provided by Parliament such expenses incurred by—

(*a*) the Central Council,

(*b*) any standing advisory committee constituted under section 6 above,

(c) the Medical Practices Committee,

(d) the Tribunal constituted under section 46 above, and

(e) the Dental Estimates Board,

as may be determined by the Secretary of State with the approval of the Treasury.

(2) Payments made under this section shall be in accordance with regulations made by the Secretary of State and approved by the Treasury, and shall be made at such times and in such manner as the Treasury may direct, and subject to such conditions as to records, certificates, or otherwise as the Secretary of State may with the approval of the Treasury determine.

**101.** Any sums received by the Secretary of State under this Act shall be paid into the Consolidated Fund, but this section is without prejudice to section 60(4) above.

Secretary of State's receipts.

*Miscellaneous provisions as to remuneration,*
*allowances and superannuation*

**102.**—(1) The Secretary of State may pay such travelling and other allowances, including compensation for loss of remunerative time, as he may, with the approval of the Minister for the Civil Service, determine—

Allowances and remuneration for members of certain bodies.

(a) to members of any of the following bodies constituted under this Act—

(i) the Central Council, any standing advisory committee constituted under section 6 above to advise the Secretary of State and that Council, any committee appointed by that Council under paragraph 4 of Schedule 4 to this Act and any sub-committee appointed by any such standing advisory committee under that paragraph;

(ii) the Medical Practices Committee;

(iii) any body on which functions are conferred by regulations under section 32 above;

(iv) the Dental Estimates Board;

(v) the Tribunal constituted under section 46 above;

(b) to members of any other body being a body specified in an order made by the Secretary of State as being a body recognised by him to have been formed for the purpose of performing a function connected with the provision of services under this Act.

C

(2) The Secretary of State may pay to members of any of the following bodies such remuneration as he may, with the approval of the Minister for the Civil Service, determine—

(a) the Medical Practices Committee ;

(b) any body on which functions are conferred by regulations under section 32 above ;

(c) the Dental Estimates Board ;

(d) the Tribunal constituted under section 46 above ;

(e) any other body constituted under Part II of this Act, being a body specified in an order made for the purposes of this subsection, with the approval of the Minister for the Civil Service, by the Secretary of State.

(3) Allowances shall not be paid under subsection (1) above except in connection with the exercise or performance of such powers or duties, in such circumstances, as may, with the approval of the Minister for the Civil Service, be determined by the Secretary of State.

(4) Any payments under this section shall be made at such times and in such manner, and subject to such conditions as to records, certificates or otherwise, as the Secretary of State may, with the approval of the Minister for the Civil Service, determine.

Special arrangement as to payment of remuneration.

**103.**—(1) If the Secretary of State—

(a) considers it appropriate for remuneration in respect of services provided by any person in pursuance of Part II of this Act to be paid by a particular body, and

(b) apart from this section the functions of the body do not include the function of paying the remuneration,

the Secretary of State may by order confer that function on the body.

(2) Any sums required to enable any body having that function to pay remuneration in respect of such services shall, if apart from this section there is no provision authorising the payment of the sums by the Secretary of State or out of money provided by Parliament, be paid by him.

Superannuation of officers of certain hospitals.

**104.**—(1) The Secretary of State may enter into an agreement with the governing body of any hospital to which this section applies—

(a) for admitting officers of the hospital of such classes as may be provided in the agreement to participate, on such terms and conditions as may be so provided, in the superannuation benefits provided under regulations

made under section 10 of the Superannuation Act 1972
in like manner as officers of Area Health Authorities ;
and

(b) those regulations shall apply accordingly in relation to
the officers so admitted subject to such modifications
as may be provided in the agreement.

(2) The governing body of any hospital to which this section
applies shall have all such powers as may be necessary for the
purpose of giving effect to any terms and conditions on which
their officers are admitted to participate in those superannuation
benefits.

(3) This section applies to any hospital (not vested in the
Secretary of State) which is used, in pursuance of arrangements
made by the governing body of the hospital with the Secretary
of State, for the provision of services under this Act.

**105.**—(1) Where a medical practitioner carries out a medical Payments for
examination of any person with a view to an application for his certain medical
admission to hospital for observation or treatment being made examinations.
under Part IV of the Mental Health Act 1959 the council which 1959 c. 72.
is the local authority for the purposes of the Local Authority 1970 c. 42.
Social Services Act 1970 for the area where the person examined
resides shall, subject to the following provisions of this section,
pay to that medical practitioner—

(a) reasonable remuneration in respect of that examination
and in respect of any recommendation or report made
by him with regard to the person examined ; and

(b) the amount of any expenses reasonably incurred by him
in connection with the examination or the making of
any such recommendation or report.

(2) No payment shall be made under this section to a medical
practitioner—

(a) in respect of an examination carried out as part of his
duty to provide general medical services for the person
examined ; or

(b) in respect of an examination carried out or any recommendation or report made as part of his duty as an
officer of a health authority.

(3) This section shall only apply in a case where it is intended,
when the medical examination of the person in question is
carried out, that if he is admitted to hospital in pursuance of
any such application as mentioned in subsection (1) above, the
whole cost of his maintenance and treatment will be defrayed
out of moneys provided by Parliament under this Act or the
Mental Health Act 1959.

## Part V

### Health Service Commissioner for England and Health Service Commissioner for Wales

Appointment and tenure of office of Commissioners.

**106.**—(1) For the purpose of conducting investigations in accordance with this Part of this Act, there shall be appointed—

(a) a Commissioner to be known as the Health Service Commissioner for England ; and

(b) a Commissioner to be known as the Health Service Commissioner for Wales.

(2) Her Majesty may by Letters Patent from time to time appoint a person to be a Commissioner ; and a person so appointed shall, subject to subsection (3) below, hold office during good behaviour.

(3) A person appointed to be a Commissioner may be relieved of office by Her Majesty at his own request, or may be removed from office by Her Majesty in consequence of Addresses from both Houses of Parliament, and shall in any case vacate office on completing the year of service in which he attains the age of sixty-five.

(4) A person who is a member of a relevant body (within the meaning of section 109 below) shall not be appointed to be a Commissioner ; and a Commissioner shall not become a member of a relevant body.

Salaries and pensions of Commissioners.

**107.**—(1) Subject to subsections (3) and (5) below, there shall be paid to the holder of the office of a Commissioner the same salary as if he were employed in the civil service of the State in such appointment as the House of Commons may by resolution from time to time determine ; and any such resolution may take effect from the date on which it is passed, or from such other date as it may specify.

1967 c. 13.

(2) Subject to subsections (6) and (7) below, Schedule 1 to the Parliamentary Commissioner Act 1967 (which relates to pensions and other benefits) has effect with respect to persons who have held office as a Commissioner as it has effect with respect to persons who have held office as the Parliamentary Commissioner for Administration.

(3) The salary payable to a holder of the office of a Commissioner shall be abated by the amount of any pension payable to him in respect of any public office in the United Kingdom or elsewhere to which he has previously been appointed or elected.

(4) In computing the salary of a former holder of the office of Commissioner for the purposes of Schedule 1 to that Act of 1967 there shall be disregarded—

(a) any abatement of that salary under subsection (3) above ;

(b) any temporary abatement of that salary in the national interest ; and

(c) any voluntary surrender of that salary in whole or in part.

(5) Where—

(a) a person holds the office of Parliamentary Commissioner for Administration and one or more of the offices of Health Service Commissioner for England, Health Service Commissioner for Scotland and Health Service Commissioner for Wales he shall, so long as he does so, be entitled only to the salary pertaining to the first-mentioned office ; and

(b) a person holds two or more of those offices other than that of Parliamentary Commissioner for Administration he shall, so long as he does so, be entitled only to the salary pertaining to such one of those offices as he selects.

(6) A person—

(a) shall not be entitled to make simultaneously different elections in pursuance of paragraph 1 of Schedule 1 to that Act of 1967 in respect of different offices mentioned in subsection (5) above, and

(b) shall, if he has made or is treated as having made an election in pursuance of that paragraph in respect of such an office, be deemed to have made the same election in respect of all such other offices to which he is, or is subsequently, appointed,

and no account shall be taken for the purposes of that Schedule of a period of service in such an office if salary in respect of the office was not paid for that period.

(7) The Minister for the Civil Service may—

(a) by regulations provide that Schedule 1 to that Act of 1967 shall have effect in relation to persons who have held more than one of the offices mentioned in subsection (5) above, and

(b) by those regulations modify that Schedule as he considers necessary in consequence of those persons having held more than one of those offices,

and different regulations may be made in pursuance of paragraph 4 of that Schedule in relation to different offices as mentioned.

This subsection is subject to subsection (6) above.

C 3

PART V

(8) Any salary, pension or other benefit payable by virtue of this section shall be charged on and issued out of the Consolidated Fund.

Administrative
provisions.

**108.**—(1) A Commissioner may appoint such officers as he may determine with the approval of the Minister for the Civil Service as to numbers and conditions of service ; and it is the duty of the Health Service Commissioner for Wales to include among his officers such persons having a command of the Welsh language as he considers are needed to enable him to investigate complaints in Welsh.

(2) Any functions of a Commissioner under this Part of this Act may be performed by any officer of the Commissioner authorised by him for that purpose, or by any officer so authorised of another Commissioner mentioned in section 107(5) above.

(3) To assist him in any investigation, a Commissioner may obtain advice from any person who, in his opinion, is qualified to give it, and may pay such fees or allowances to any such person as he may determine with the approval of the Minister for the Civil Service.

(4) The expenses of a Commissioner under this Part of this Act, to such amount as may be sanctioned by the Minister for the Civil Service, shall be defrayed out of money provided by Parliament.

Bodies
subject to
investigation.

**109.** In this Part of this Act " relevant body " means any of the following bodies—

(a) Regional Health Authorities ;

(b) Area Health Authorities ;

(c) any special health authority established on or before 1st April 1974 ;

(d) any special health authority established after that 1st April and designated by Order in Council as an authority to which this section applies ;

(e) Family Practitioner Committees ;

(f) the Public Health Laboratory Service Board ; and

(g) the Health Services Board and its Welsh Committee.

Except where the context otherwise requires, any reference in this Part of this Act to a relevant body includes a reference to an officer of the body.

**110.** The Health Service Commissioner for England shall not conduct an investigation under this Part of this Act in respect of—

PART V
Investigations
for England,
and for Wales.

(a) an Area Health Authority of which the area is in Wales,

(b) the Family Practitioner Committee established by such an Authority,

(c) a special health authority exercising functions only or mainly in Wales, or

(d) the Welsh Committee of the Health Services Board,

and the Health Service Commissioner for Wales shall not conduct such an investigation in respect of a relevant body other than one of those bodies.

**111.**—(1) A complaint under this Part of this Act may be made by any individual, or by any body of persons whether incorporated or not, not being—

Who may complain.

(a) a local authority or other authority or body constituted for purposes of the public service or of local government, or for the purposes of carrying on under national ownership any industry or undertaking or part of an industry or undertaking;

(b) any other authority or body whose members are appointed by Her Majesty or any Minister of the Crown or government department, or whose revenues consist wholly or mainly of money provided by Parliament.

(2) Where the person by whom a complaint might have been made under the preceding provisions of this Part has died, or is for any reason unable to act for himself, the complaint may be made—

(a) by his personal representative, or

(b) by a member of his family, or

(c) by some body or individual suitable to represent him,

but, except as aforesaid and as provided by section 117 below, a complaint shall not be entertained under this Part unless made by the person aggrieved himself.

**112.** Before proceeding to investigate a complaint—

Reply.

(a) a Commissioner shall satisfy himself that the complaint has been brought by or on behalf of the person aggrieved to the notice of the relevant body in question, and that that body had been afforded a reasonable opportunity to investigate and reply to the complaint, but

C 4

PART V    (*b*) a Commissioner shall disregard the provisions of paragraph (*a*) in relation to a complaint made by an officer of the relevant body in question on behalf of the person aggrieved if the officer is authorised by virtue of section 111(2) above to make the complaint and the Commissioner is satisfied that in the particular circumstances those provisions ought to be disregarded.

Commissioner's discretion.

**113.**—(1) In determining whether to initiate, continue or discontinue an investigation under this Part of this Act, a Commissioner shall, subject to section 110 above and sections 115 and 116 below, act in accordance with his own discretion.

(2) Any question whether a complaint is duly made to a Commissioner under this Part shall be determined by the Commissioner.

Procedure, and additional procedural provisions.

**114.**—(1) A Commissioner—

(*a*) shall not entertain a complaint under this Part of this Act unless it is made in writing to him by or on behalf of the person aggrieved not later than one year from the day on which the person aggrieved first had notice of the matters alleged in the complaint, but

(*b*) may conduct an investigation pursuant to a complaint not made within that period if he considers it reasonable to do so.

(2) The additional provisions contained in Part I of Schedule 13 to this Act, which relate to procedure and other matters, have effect for the purposes of this Part.

Matters subject to investigation.

**115.** A Commissioner may investigate—

(*a*) an alleged failure in a service provided by a relevant body, or

(*b*) an alleged failure of such a body to provide a service which it was a function of the body to provide, or

(*c*) any other action taken by or on behalf of such a body,

in a case where a complaint is duly made by or on behalf of any person that he has sustained injustice or hardship in consequence of the failure or in consequence of maladministration connected with the other action.

This section is subject to sections 110 and 113 above and section 116 below.

**116.**—(1) Except as hereafter provided, a Commissioner shall not conduct an investigation under this Part of this Act in respect of any of the following matters—

PART V
Matters not subject to investigation.

    (*a*) any action in respect of which the person aggrieved has or had a right of appeal, reference or review to or before a tribunal constituted by or under any enactment or by virtue of Her Majesty's prerogative, or

    (*b*) any action in respect of which the person aggrieved has or had a remedy by way of proceedings in any court of law,

but a Commissioner may conduct an investigation notwithstanding that the person aggrieved has or had such a right or remedy, if satisfied that in the particular circumstances it is not reasonable to expect him to resort or have resorted to it.

(2) Without prejudice to subsection (1) above—

    (*a*) a Commissioner shall not conduct an investigation under this Part in respect of any such action as is described in Part II of Schedule 13 to this Act; and

    (*b*) nothing in sections 110, 113 and 115 above shall be construed as authorising such an investigation in respect of action taken in connection with any general medical services, general dental services, general ophthalmic services or pharmaceutical services by a person providing the services.

(3) Her Majesty may by Order in Council amend Part II of Schedule 13 so as to exclude from it action described in sub-paragraph (3) or (4) of paragraph 19 of that Schedule.

**117.** Notwithstanding anything in sections 111 and 112 and section 114(1) above, a relevant body—

Reference to Commissioner by relevant body.

    (*a*) may itself (excluding its officers) refer to a Commissioner a complaint that a person has, in consequence of a failure or maladministration for which the body is responsible, sustained such injustice or hardship as is mentioned in section 115 above if the complaint—

        (i) is made in writing to the relevant body by that person, or by a person authorised by virtue of section 111(2) above to make the complaint to the Commissioner on his behalf, and

        (ii) is so made not later than one year from the day mentioned in section 114(1) above, or within such other period as the Commissioner considers appropriate in any particular case, but

    (*b*) shall not be entitled to refer a complaint in pursuance of paragraph (*a*) after the expiry of three months beginning with the day on which the body received the complaint.

A complaint referred to a Commissioner in pursuance of this section shall, subject to section 113 above, be deemed to be duly made to him under this Part of this Act.

Consultations
between
Commissioners
and Local
Commis-
sioners.

1974 c. 7.

**118.**—(1) Where, at any stage in the course of conducting an investigation under this Part of this Act, the Commissioner conducting the investigation—

(a) forms the opinion that the complaint relates partly to a matter which could be the subject of an investigation under Part III of the Local Government Act 1974, then

(b) he shall consult about the complaint with the appropriate Local Commissioner within the meaning of Part III of that Act of 1974, and

(c) if he considers it necessary, inform the person initiating the complaint under this Part of the steps necessary to initiate a complaint under Part III of that Act of 1974.

(2) Where under subsection (1) above a Commissioner consults with a Local Commissioner in relation to a complaint under this Part of this Act, he may consult that Commissioner about any matter relating to the complaint, including—

(a) the conduct of any investigation into the complaint; and

(b) the form, content and publication of any report of the results of such an investigation.

(3) Nothing in paragraph 16 of Schedule 13 to this Act applies in relation to the disclosure of information by a Commissioner or his officers in the course of consultations held in accordance with this section.

Reports by
Commis-
sioners.

**119.**—(1) In any case where a Commissioner conducts an investigation under this Part of this Act, he shall send a report of the results of his investigation—

(a) to the person who made the complaint,

(b) to the relevant body in question,

(c) to any person who is alleged in the complaint to have taken or authorised the action complained of,

(d) if the relevant body in question is not an Area Health Authority for an area in England or a Family Practitioner Committee, to the Secretary of State,

(e) if that body is an Area Health Authority for an area in England, to the Regional Health Authority of which the region includes that area, and

(f) if that body is a Family Practitioner Committee, to the Area Health Authority by which the Committee was established,

but paragraph (d) does not apply in the case of an investigation conducted in respect of the Health Services Board or the Welsh Committee unless the Commissioner thinks fit to publish his report under this subsection.

(2) In any case where a Commissioner decides not to conduct an investigation under this Part, he shall send a statement of his reasons for doing so to the person who made the complaint and to the relevant body in question.

(3) If, after conducting an investigation under this Part, it appears to a Commissioner that the person aggrieved has sustained such injustice or hardship as is mentioned in section 115 above, and that the injustice or hardship has not been and will not be remedied, he may if he thinks fit—

(a) in relation to an investigation conducted in respect of the Health Services Board or the Welsh Committee, lay before each House of Parliament a special report;

(b) in relation to any other investigation, make a special report to the Secretary of State who shall, as soon as is reasonably practicable, lay a copy of the report before each House of Parliament.

(4) Each of the Commissioners shall—

(a) annually lay before each House of Parliament a general report on the performance of his functions under this Part in respect of the Health Services Board and the Welsh Committee, and may from time to time lay before each House of Parliament such other reports with respect to those functions as he thinks fit;

(b) annually make to the Secretary of State a report on the performance of his other functions under this Part, and may from time to time make to the Secretary of State such other reports with respect to those functions as the Commissioner thinks fit, and the Secretary of State shall lay a copy of every such report before each House of Parliament.

(5) For the purposes of the law of defamation, the publication of any matter by a Commissioner in sending or making a report in pursuance of subsection (1), (3) or (4) above, or in sending a statement in pursuance of subsection (2) above, shall be absolutely privileged.

**120.**—(1) In this Part of this Act and in Schedule 13 to this Act— *Interpretation of Part V.*

" action " includes failure to act, and other expressions connoting action shall be construed accordingly;

PART V

" Commissioner " means the Health Service Commissioner for England or the Health Service Commissioner for Wales, and " Commissioners " means both those persons ;

" person aggrieved " means the person who claims or is alleged to have sustained such injustice or hardship as is mentioned in section 115 above ; and

" relevant body " has the meaning given by section 109 above, and (except where the context otherwise requires) includes a reference to an officer of the body.

(2) Nothing in this Part of this Act authorises or requires a Commissioner to question the merits of a decision taken without maladministration by a relevant body in the exercise of a discretion vested in that body.

## PART VI

### MISCELLANEOUS AND SUPPLEMENTARY

*General provisions as to charges*

Charges in respect of non-residents.

**121.** Regulations may provide for the making and recovery, in such manner as may be prescribed, of such charges—

(a) in respect of such services provided under this Act as may be prescribed, being

(b) services provided in respect of such persons not ordinarily resident in Great Britain as may be prescribed.

Such regulations may provide that the charges are only to be made in such cases as may be determined in accordance with the regulations.

Recovery of charges.

**122.**—(1) All charges recoverable under this Act by the Secretary of State, a local social services authority, or any body constituted under this Act, may, without prejudice to any other method of recovery, be recovered summarily as a civil debt.

(2) If any person, for the purpose of evading the payment of any charge under this Act, or of reducing the amount of any such charge—

(a) knowingly makes any false statement or false representation, or

(b) produces or furnishes, or causes or knowingly allows to be produced or furnished, any document or information which he knows to be false in a material particular,

the charge, or as the case may be the balance of the charge, may be recovered from him as a simple contract debt by the person by whom the cost of the service in question was defrayed.

**123.**—(1) Where the carrying out of a scheme for the provision Persons
by the Secretary of State in pursuance of this Act of hospital displaced by
accommodation or other facilities will involve the displacement development.
from any premises of persons residing in them, the Secretary of
State may make arrangements with one or more of the following
bodies—

    (a) an authority who are a local authority for the purposes
        of the Housing Act 1957, 1957 c. 56.

    (b) a housing association within the meaning of that Act of
        1957,

    (c) a housing trust within the meaning of that Act of 1957,

    (d) a development corporation established under the New 1965 c. 59.
        Towns Act 1965, and

    (e) the Commission for the New Towns,

for securing, in so far as it appears to him that there is no
other residential accommodation suitable for the reasonable
requirements of those persons available on reasonable terms, the
provision of residential accommodation in advance of the displacement from time to time becoming necessary as the carrying
out of the scheme proceeds.

(2) Arrangements under subsection (1) above may include
provision for the making by the Secretary of State to the body
with whom the arrangements are made of payments of such
amounts and for such purposes as may be approved by the
Treasury.

**124.**—(1) The requirements of this section with respect to the Special notices
notification of births and deaths are in addition to, and not in of births
substitution for, the requirements of any Act relating to the and deaths.
registration of births and deaths.

(2) It is the duty of each registrar of births and deaths to
furnish, to the prescribed medical officer of the Area Health
Authority of which the area includes the whole or part of the
registrar's sub-district, such particulars of each birth and death
which occurred in the Authority's area as are entered (on and
after 1st April 1974) in a register of births or deaths kept for
that sub-district.

(3) Regulations may provide as to the manner in which and
the times at which particulars are to be furnished in pursuance
of subsection (2) above.

(4) In the case of every child born, it is the duty—

    (a) of the child's father, if at the time of the birth he is
        actually residing on the premises where the birth takes
        place, and

(*b*) of any person in attendance upon the mother at the time of, or within six hours after, the birth,

to give notice of the birth (as provided in subsection (5) below) to the prescribed medical officer of the Area Health Authority for the area in which the birth takes place.

This subsection applies to any child which has issued forth from its mother after the expiry of the twenty-eighth week of pregnancy whether alive or dead.

(5) Notice under subsection (4) above shall be given either—

(*a*) by posting within 36 hours after the birth a prepaid letter or postcard addressed to the prescribed medical officer of the Area Health Authority at his office and containing the required information, or

(*b*) by delivering within that period at that officer's office a written notice containing the required information,

and an Area Health Authority shall, upon application to them, supply without charge to any medical practitioner or midwife residing or practising within their area prepaid addressed envelopes together with the forms of notice.

(6) Any person who fails to give notice of a birth in accordance with subsection (4) above is liable on summary conviction to a fine not exceeding £1, unless he satisfies the court that he believed, and had reasonable grounds for believing, that notice had been duly given by some other person.

Proceedings in respect of this offence shall not, without the Attorney-General's written consent, be taken by any person other than a party aggrieved or the Area Health Authority concerned.

(7) A registrar of births and deaths shall, for the purpose of obtaining information concerning births which have occurred in his sub-district, have access at all reasonable times to notices of births received by a medical officer under this section, or to any book in which those notices may be recorded.

Protection of members and officers of authorities.
1875 c. 55.

**125.** Section 265 of the Public Health Act 1875 (which relates to the protection of members and officers of certain authorities) has effect as if there were included in the authorities referred to in that section—

(*a*) a Regional Health Authority,

(*b*) an Area Health Authority,

(*c*) a special health authority, and

(*d*) a Family Practitioner Committee,

and as if any reference in that section to the Public Health Act 1875 included a reference to this Act.

*Supplementary*

**126.**—(1) Any power to make orders or regulations conferred Orders and
by this Act shall be exercisable by statutory instrument, and a regulations,
statutory instrument made by virtue of this Act shall be subject and directions
to annulment in pursuance of a resolution of either House of
Parliament.

This subsection—

(*a*) is subject to paragraph 15(3) of Schedule 5 to this Act ;

(*b*) does not apply to paragraph 10 of Schedule 11 to this
    Act.

(2) Any power to make regulations conferred on the Secretary
of State by this Act is, if the Treasury so directs, exercisable
by the Treasury and the Secretary of State acting jointly, except
in the case of—

(*a*) regulations made under section 32 above ;

(*b*) regulations made under section 77(1) above in respect
    of charges for the drugs, medicines or appliances
    referred to in paragraph (*a*) of that subsection, or
    under paragraph 1(1) of Schedule 12 to this Act in
    respect of the remission or repayment of any charge
    payable under that section in the cases provided for
    in paragraph 1(1) of that Schedule ;

(*c*) regulations made under paragraph 2(2) of that Schedule ;

(*d*) regulations made under paragraph 2(6) of that Schedule.

(3) Where under any provision of this Act—

(*a*) power to make an order may be exercisable, or

(*b*) directions may be given,

that provision includes power to vary or revoke the order or
direction, as the case may be, by subsequent order or by
subsequent directions.

In relation to directions given by the Secretary of State in
pursuance of sections 13 to 17 above this subsection is subject
to section 18 above.

(4) Any power conferred by this Act to make orders, regulations or schemes, and any power conferred by section 18 above
to give directions by an instrument in writing, may, unless the
contrary intention appears, be exercised—

(*a*) either in relation to all cases to which the power extends,
    or in relation to all those cases subject to specified
    exceptions, or in relation to any specified cases or
    classes of case, and

(*b*) so as to make, as respects the cases in relation to which
    it is exercised—

    (i) the full provision to which the power extends
    or any less provision (whether by way of exception
    or otherwise),

(ii) the same provision for all cases in relation to which the power is exercised, or different provision for different cases or different classes of case, or different provision as respects the same case or class of case for different purposes of this Act or that section,

(iii) any such provision either unconditionally, or subject to any specified condition,

and includes power to make such incidental or supplemental provision in the orders, regulations, schemes or directions as the persons making or giving them consider appropriate.

This subsection does not apply to regulations made under section 32 above (but without prejudice to subsection (3) of that section) or to an order made under section 57 above (but without prejudice to paragraph 1(1) of Schedule 11 to this Act).

Supplementary regulatory powers.

**127.** Regulations may provide for all or any of the following matters—

(a) for prescribing the forms and manner of service of notices and other documents ;

(b) for prescribing the manner in which documents may be executed or proved ;

(c) for prescribing the manner in which resolutions of any bodies (except the Public Health Laboratory Service Board) continued in being by this Act are to be proved ;

(d) for exempting judges and justices of the peace from disqualification by their liability to rates.

Interpretation and construction.

**128.**—(1) In this Act, unless the contrary intention appears—

" the Central Council" means the Central Health Services Council referred to in section 6 above ;

1951 c. 53.

" certified midwife " means a person who is for the time being certified under the Midwives Act 1951 ;

1957 c. 28.

" dental practitioner " means a person registered in the dentists register under the Dentists Act 1957 ;

1958 c. 32.

" dispensing optician " means a person who is registered in the register kept under section 2 of the Opticians Act 1958 of dispensing opticians or a body corporate enrolled in the list kept under section 4 of that Act of such bodies carrying on business as dispensing opticians ;

" equipment " includes any machinery, apparatus or appliance, whether fixed or not, and any vehicle ;

" functions " includes powers and duties ;

" health authority " means a Regional or Area Health Authority or a special health authority ;

" **the** health service " means the health service established   
in pursuance of section 1(1) above ;

" **health** service hospital " means a hospital vested in the
Secretary of State under this Act ;

" Health Services Board " means the body established by
section 1 of the Health Services Act 1976 ;     1976 c. 83.

" hospital " means—

    (*a*) any institution for the reception and treatment
of persons suffering from illness,

    (*b*) any maternity home, and

    (*c*) any institution for the reception and treatment
of persons during convalescence or persons requiring
medical rehabilitation,

and includes clinics, dispensaries and out-patient
departments maintained in connection with any such
home or institution, and " hospital accommodation "
shall be construed accordingly ;

" illness " includes mental disorder within the meaning of
the Mental Health Act 1959 and any injury or dis- 1959 c. 72.
ability requiring medical or dental treatment or
nursing ;

" local authority " means a county council, the Greater
London Council, a district council, a London borough
council, and the Common Council of the City of
London ; and includes the King Edward VII Welsh
National Memorial Association ;

" local education authority " has the same meaning as in the
Education Act 1944 ;     1944 c. 31.

" local social services authority " means the council of a
non-metropolitan county, or of a metropolitan district
or London borough, or the Common Council of the
City of London ;

" medical " includes surgical ;

" medical practitioner " means a fully registered person
within the meaning of the Medical Act 1956 ;     1956 c. 76.

" medicine " includes such chemical re-agents as are
included in a list for the time being approved by the
Secretary of State for the purposes of section 41 above ;

" modifications " includes additions, omissions and amendments ;

" officer " includes servant ;

" ophthalmic optician " means a person registered in either
of the registers kept under section 2 of the Opticians 1958 c. 32.
Act 1958 of ophthalmic opticians or a body corporate
enrolled in the list kept under section 4 of that Act of

1919 c. 94.

1957 c. 15.

PART VI

such bodies carrying on business as ophthalmic opticians;

" patient " includes an expectant or nursing mother and a lying-in woman;

" prescribed " means prescribed by regulations made by the Secretary of State under this Act;

" property " includes rights;

" registered nurse " means a nurse registered in the register of nurses established under the Nurses Registration Act 1919 and maintained in pursuance of section 2(1) of the Nurses Act 1957;

" registered pharmacist " means a pharmacist registered in the register of pharmaceutical chemists;

" regulations " means regulations made by the Secretary of State under this Act;

" special hospital " has the meaning given by section 4 above;

" superannuation benefits " means annual superannuation allowances, gratuities and periodical payments payable on retirement, death or incapacity, and similar benefits;

" university " includes a university college;

" voluntary " means not carried on for profit and not provided by a local or public authority;

1976 c. 83.

" Welsh Committee " means the committee constituted under section 1(3) of the Health Services Act 1976.

(2) References in this Act to the purposes of a hospital shall be construed as referring both to the general purposes of the hospital and to any specific purpose of the hospital.

(3) Any reference in this Act to any enactment is a reference to it as amended or applied by or under any other enactment including this Act.

Transitional provisions and savings, consequential amendments, and repeals.

**129.** Schedule 14 to this Act is hereby given effect, and subject to the transitional provisions and savings contained in that Schedule—

(a) the enactments and the Order specified in Schedule 15 to this Act have effect subject to the amendments (being amendments consequent on this Act) specified in that Schedule, and

(b) the enactments specified in Schedule 16 to this Act (which include enactments which were spent before the passing of this Act) are hereby repealed to the extent specified in the third column of that Schedule,

but nothing in this Act shall be taken as prejudicing the operation of section 38 of the Interpretation Act 1889 (which relates to the operation of repeals).

1889 c. 63.

**130.**—(1) This Act may be cited as the National Health
Service Act 1977.

(2) This Act does not extend to Scotland, except as is mentioned in paragraph 3 of Schedule 11 to this Act.

(3) The following provisions only of this Act apply to Northern Ireland—

    (*a*) this subsection and subsections (1) above and (5) below ;

    (*b*) section 57 above and Schedule 11 to this Act ;

    (*ċ*) section 114(2) above and Part I of Schedule 13 to this Act, section 119(5) above, and section 120(1) above so far as it relates to the provisions mentioned in this paragraph ;

    (*d*) paragraph 13 of Schedule 14 to this Act so far as it relates to any enactment which extends to Northern Ireland ;

    (*e*) paragraph (*a*) of section 129 above and Schedule 15 to this Act so far as they amend any enactment and order which extends to Northern Ireland ;

    (*f*) paragraph (*b*) of section 129 and Schedule 16 to this Act so far as they repeal any enactment which extends to Northern Ireland.

(4) The Secretary of State may by order provide that this Act shall extend to the Isles of Scilly with such modifications, if any, as are specified in the order, and except as provided in pursuance of this subsection this Act does not extend to the Isles of Scilly.

The Secretary of State may by any such order amend or repeal any provisions contained in the Isles of Scilly Orders 1927 to 1943.

(5) This Act shall come into force on the expiry of the period of one month beginning on the date of its passing.

# SCHEDULES

Section 5(1).

## SCHEDULE 1

### ADDITIONAL PROVISIONS AS TO THE MEDICAL AND DENTAL INSPECTION AND TREATMENT OF PUPILS

1. Without prejudice to the Secretary of State's powers apart from this paragraph, he may—

    (*a*) by arrangement with any local education authority, provide for any medical or dental inspection or treatment of—

        (i) senior pupils in attendance at any educational establishment, other than a school, which is maintained by the authority and at which full-time further education is provided, or

        (ii) any child or young person who, in pursuance of special arrangements made for him by the authority by virtue of section 56 of the Education Act 1944, is receiving primary or secondary education otherwise than at a school ;

    (*b*) by arrangement with the proprietor of any educational establishment which is not maintained by a local education authority, make any such provision in respect of junior or senior pupils in attendance at the establishment.

1944 c. 31.

2. A local education authority shall not arrange in pursuance of paragraph 1 above in respect of such an establishment as is mentioned in sub-paragraph (*a*)(i) of that paragraph except by agreement with the governors of the establishment ; and an arrangement in pursuance of sub-paragraph (*b*) of paragraph 1 may provide for payments by the proprietor in question.

3. It is the duty of the local education authorities by which schools (other than voluntary schools) are maintained and of the managers or governors of voluntary schools to make available to the Secretary of State such accommodation as is appropriate for the purpose of assisting him so to provide as is mentioned in paragraph (*a*) of section 5(1) above for pupils in attendance at the schools.

4. In paragraph (*a*) of section 5(1) above, and in this Schedule expressions to which meanings are given by section 114(1) of the Education Act 1944 have those meanings.

Section 5(2).

## SCHEDULE 2

### ADDITIONAL PROVISIONS AS TO VEHICLES FOR THOSE SUFFERING DISABILITY

1. The Secretary of State has power, in the case of an invalid carriage or other vehicle provided by him for or belonging to any such person as is mentioned in paragraph (*a*) of section 5(2) above, on such terms and subject to such conditions as he may determine—

    (*a*) to adapt the vehicle for the purposes of making it suitable for the circumstances of that person ;

(*b*) to maintain and repair the vehicle ;    

(*c*) to take out insurance policies relating to the vehicle and pay the duty, if any, with which the vehicle is chargeable under the Vehicles (Excise) Act 1971 ;    

(*d*) to provide a structure in which the vehicle may be kept, and to provide all material and execute all works necessary for the structure's erection.

2. The Secretary of State may, on such terms and subject to such conditions as he may determine, make payments by way of grant towards costs incurred by any such person as is mentioned in paragraph (*a*) of section 5(2) above in respect of all or any of the following matters in relation to an invalid carriage or other vehicle provided by the Secretary of State for or belonging to that person—

(*a*) the taking of any such action as is referred to in paragraph 1 above ;

(*b*) the purchase of fuel for the purposes of the vehicle, so far as the cost of the purchase is attributable to duties of excise payable in respect of the fuel ; and

(*c*) the taking of instruction in the driving of the vehicle.

3. Regulations may provide for any incidental or supplementary matter for which it appears to the Secretary of State necessary or expedient to provide in connection with the taking of action under paragraph 1 above or the making of any payment under paragraph 2 above.

4. In paragraph (*a*) of section 5(2) above, and in this Schedule, " invalid carriage " means a mechanically propelled vehicle specially designed and constructed (and not merely adapted) for the use of a person suffering some physical defect or disability and used solely by such a person.

## SCHEDULE 3    

### Public Health Laboratory Service Board

### Part I

### Constitution of the Public Health Laboratory Service Board

1. The Public Health Laboratory Service Board shall be a body corporate.

2. The Board may accept, hold and administer property on trust for any purposes relating to the public health laboratory service or otherwise connected with microbiological research.

3. The Board shall consist of a chairman appointed by the Secretary of State and such other members so appointed as the Secretary of State thinks fit, and the members shall include—

(*a*) not less than two persons appointed after consultation with the Medical Research Council ; and

SCH. 3

(b) not less than two persons with experience as microbiologists, appointed after consultation with such organisations as the Secretary of State thinks appropriate ; and

(c) not less than two proper officers appointed by a local authority ; and

(d) not less than one person with experience of service in hospitals ; and

(e) not less than one medical practitioner engaged in general medical practice, appointed after consultation with such organisations as the Secretary of State may recognise as representative of practitioners so engaged.

4. Subject to paragraph 5 below members shall be appointed for a term of three years.

5. Any member appointed to fill a casual vacancy shall be appointed for the remainder of the term for which his predecessor was appointed.

6. A member may at any time resign his office.

7. A person who is or has been a member of the Board shall be eligible for re-appointment as a member.

8. The Board may elect a deputy chairman and may appoint one or more committees consisting wholly or partly of members of the Board and may delegate to any such committee any of the Board's functions.

9. The proceedings of the Board or any committee appointed by the Board shall not be invalidated by any vacancy in the membership of the Board or committee, or by any defect in the appointment or qualification of any such member.

10. The Board and, subject to any directions of the Board, any committee appointed by them, may regulate their own procedure and fix a quorum for any of their proceedings.

## PART II

### ADDITIONAL PROVISIONS AS TO THE PUBLIC HEALTH LABORATORY SERVICE BOARD

11. The Board may appoint such officers and servants, on such terms as to remuneration and conditions of service, as the Board may, with the Secretary of State's approval, determine.

12. The Board may pay to its members and to the members of any committee appointed by the Board such travelling and other allowances, including compensation for loss of remunerative time, as the Board may, with the approval of the Secretary of State and the Minister for the Civil Service, determine.

SCH. 3

13. The Board shall exercise their functions in accordance with any direction which the Secretary of State may give to them but shall in the exercise of those functions be deemed for all purposes to act as principal.

14. The Secretary of State shall pay to the Board, out of moneys provided by Parliament, such sums as may be necessary to defray the expenditure of the Board incurred with his approval.

15. Any sums received by the Board (otherwise than in exercise of their power under paragraph 2 above, or under paragraph 14 above) shall be paid into the Consolidated Fund.

16. The Board shall keep proper accounts and other records in such form as the Secretary of State may, with the approval of the Treasury, determine.

17. The Board shall prepare and transmit to the Secretary of State in respect of each financial year statements of account in such form as the Secretary of State may, with the approval of the Treasury, determine.

18. The Secretary of State shall transmit these statements of accounts on or before 30th November following the financial year to the Comptroller and Auditor General, who shall examine and certify them and lay copies of them together with his report on them before each House of Parliament.

## SCHEDULE 4

Section 6.

### CENTRAL HEALTH SERVICES COUNCIL AND ADVISORY COMMITTEES

#### *Constitution of Central Council*

1.—(1) The number of members of the Central Council shall be not less than forty, and not more than forty-four, of whom—

  (a) thirteen shall be nominated members in accordance with sub-paragraph (2) below ;

  (b) twenty-seven shall be selected members in accordance with sub-paragraph (5) below ; and

  (c) the remaining members shall be such persons appointed by the Secretary of State as he thinks fit.

(2) The nominated members of the Central Council shall be—

  (a) the persons for the time being holding the offices of—

  The President of the Royal College of Physicians of London ;

  The President of the Royal College of Surgeons of England ;

  The President of the Royal College of Obstetricians and Gynae-cologists ;

  The President of the Royal College of Psychiatrists ;

  The President of the Royal College of Pathologists ;

The President of the Royal College of General Practitioners ;

The President of the Royal College of Nursing and National Council of Nurses of the United Kingdom ;

The President of the Royal College of Midwives ;

The Chairman of the Council of the British Medical Association ;

The Chairman of the Council of the British Dental Association ;

The President of the Faculty of Community Medicine ;

The President of the Pharmaceutical Society of Great Britain ; and

(b) one member of the Personal Social Services Council nominated by that body.

(3) Any office-holder specified in paragraph (a) of sub-paragraph (2) above may notify the Secretary of State in writing of another member of the body in which he holds office who is to be a member of the Central Council in his place for such period or any part of such period as he holds that office.

(4) The person of whom such notification is given shall be a member of the Central Council—

(a) until he resigns ; or

(b) until the office-holder ceases to hold office ; or

(c) until the office-holder notifies the Secretary of State in writing that he wishes some other person to be a member in his place or that he wishes to be a member himself.

(5) The selected members of the Central Council, who shall be appointed by the Secretary of State, shall be—

(a) eight medical practitioners ;

(b) two dental practitioners ;

(c) three registered nurses or certified midwives ;

(d) one registered pharmacist ;

(e) one registered optician ;

(f) seven persons with experience in health service management ;

(g) one person with qualifications or experience in social work ; and

(h) four persons, who, in the opinion of the Secretary of State, are interested in the health service from the point of view of members of the public.

Before appointing any of the persons specified in paragraphs (a) to (g) respectively, the Secretary of State shall consult with such organisations as he may recognise as representative of such persons, and before appointing the persons specified in paragraph (h) he shall consult with such bodies as appear to him to be appropriate for this purpose.

*Supplementary provisions*

2. Regulations may make provision with respect to the appointment, tenure of office and vacation of office of the members of the Central Council, and of any standing advisory committee constituted under section 6 above.

3. The Secretary of State shall appoint a secretary to the Central Council and to each standing advisory committee.

4. The Central Council may appoint such committees, and any standing advisory committee may appoint such sub-committees, as they think fit, and as are approved by the Secretary of State, to consider and report upon questions referred to them by the Central Council or standing advisory committee as the case may be.

Any such committee or sub-committee may include persons who are not members of the Central Council or standing advisory committee as the case may be.

5. The Central Council and any standing advisory committee shall elect one of the members of the Council or committee as the case may be to be chairman of the Council or committee, and shall have power to regulate their own procedure.

6. The proceedings of the Central Council or of any standing advisory committee shall not be invalidated by any vacancy in the membership of the Council or committee, or by any defect in a member's appointment or qualification.

## SCHEDULE 5

REGIONAL AND AREA HEALTH AUTHORITIES, FAMILY PRACTITIONER COMMITTEES, AND SPECIAL HEALTH AUTHORITIES

### PART I

MEMBERSHIP OF REGIONAL AND AREA HEALTH AUTHORITIES

*Regional Health Authorities*

1.—(1) A Regional Health Authority shall consist of a chairman appointed by the Secretary of State, and of such number of other members appointed by him as he thinks fit.

(2) Except in prescribed cases, it is the Secretary of State's duty, before he appoints a member of a Regional Health Authority other than the chairman, to consult with respect to the appointment—

  (a) such of the following bodies of which the areas or parts of them are within the region of the Authority, namely, county councils, metropolitan district councils, the Greater London Council, London borough councils, and the Common Council of the City of London ;

  (b) the university or universities with which the provision of health services in that region is, or is to be, associated ;

(c) such bodies as the Secretary of State may recognise as being, either in that region or generally, representative respectively of medical practitioners, dental practitioners, nurses, midwives, registered pharmacists and ophthalmic and dispensing opticians, or representative of such other professions as appear to him to be concerned ;

(d) any federation of workers' organisations which appears to the Secretary of State to be concerned, and any voluntary organisation within the meaning of section 23 above and any other body which appear to him to be concerned ; and

(e) in the case of an appointment of a member falling to be made after the establishment of the Regional Health Authority in question, that Authority,

### Area Health Authorities

2.—(1) Subject to paragraph 4 below, an Area Health Authority for an area in England shall consist of the following members—

(a) a chairman appointed by the Secretary of State ;

(b) the specified number of members appointed by the relevant Regional Authority after consultation (except in prescribed cases) with the bodies mentioned in sub-paragraph (2) below ;

(c) the specified number of members appointed by the relevant Regional Authority on the nomination of the university or universities specified as being associated with the provision of health services in that Authority's region ; and

(d) the specified number (not less than four) of members appointed by the specified local authority or local authorities.

(2) The bodies referred to in sub-paragraph (1)(b) above are—

(a) such bodies as the relevant Regional Authority may recognise as being, either in its region or in the area of the Area Health Authority or generally, representative respectively of medical practitioners, dental practitioners, nurses, midwives, registered pharmacists and ophthalmic and dispensing opticians, or representative of such other professions as appear to the relevant Regional Authority to be concerned ;

(b) such other bodies (including any federation of workers' organisations) as appear to the relevant Regional Authority to be concerned, excluding any university which has nominated, or is entitled to nominate, a member, and any local authority which has appointed, or is entitled to appoint, a member ; and

(c) in the case of an appointment of a member falling to be made after the establishment of the Area Health Authority in question, that Authority.

3. Paragraph 2 above applies to an Area Health Authority for an area in Wales as if, for any reference to the relevant Regional Authority, there were substituted a reference to the Secretary of State, and for any reference to England or the region of that Authority there were substituted a reference to Wales.

4. The members of an Area Health Authority (Teaching) shall, in addition to the members appointed in pursuance of paragraph 2 above, include the specified number of members appointed—

    (*a*) in the case of such an Authority the area of which is in England, by the relevant Regional Authority from among persons appearing to that Authority to have knowledge of and experience in, the administration of a hospital providing substantial facilities for under-graduate or post-graduate clinical teaching ; and

    (*b*) in the case of such an Authority the area of which is in Wales, by the Secretary of State from among persons appearing to him to have such knowledge and experience.

### *Supplemental*

5.—(1) For the purposes of paragraphs 2 to 4 above—

    (*a*) " local authority " means the council of a non-metropolitan county, a metropolitan district and a London borough, the Inner London Education Authority, and the Common Council of the City of London ;

    (*b*) " the relevant Regional Authority " means the Regional Health Authority of which the region includes the area of the Area Health Authority in question ; and

    (*c*) " specified " means specified in the order establishing the Area Health Authority in question, or, where another order provides for it to be called an Area Health Authority (Teaching), in that other order.

(2) Where—

    (*a*) an order establishing an Area Health Authority, or another order providing for it to be called an Area Health Authority or an Area Health Authority (Teaching), specifies more than one university in pursuance of paragraph 2(1)(*c*) above, the order may contain provision as to which of the universities shall (either severally or jointly) nominate all or any of the members falling to be nominated in pursuance of that provision ;

    (*b*) such an order specifies more than one local authority in pursuance of paragraph 2(1)(*d*) above, the order may provide for each of the local authorities to appoint in pursuance of paragraph 2(1)(*d*) the number of members specified in the order in relation to that local authority.

PART II

MEMBERSHIP OF FAMILY PRACTITIONER COMMITTEES

6.—(1) Subject to paragraph 7 below, a Family Practitioner Committee shall consist of thirty members, of whom—

(a) eleven shall be appointed by the Area Health Authority responsible for establishing the Committee, and at least one of them must be, but not every one of them shall be, a member of the Authority ;

(b) four shall be appointed by the local authority entitled in pursuance of paragraph 2(1)(d) above to appoint members of that Authority or, where two or more local authorities are so entitled, by those authorities acting jointly ;

(c) eight shall be appointed by the Local Medical Committee for the area of that Authority, and one of them must be, but not more than one of them shall be, a medical practitioner having the qualifications prescribed in pursuance of section 38 above (ophthalmic services) ;

(d) three shall be appointed by the Local Dental Committee for that area ;

(e) two shall be appointed by the Local Pharmaceutical Committee for that area ;

(f) one shall be an ophthalmic optician appointed by such members of the Local Optical Committee for that area as are ophthalmic opticians ;

(g) one shall be a dispensing optician appointed by such members of that Local Optical Committee as are dispensing opticians.

The members of a Family Practitioner Committee shall from time to time, in accordance with such procedure as may be prescribed, select one of their members to be the chairman of the Committee.

(2) If any appointment falling to be made in pursuance of sub-paragraph (1) above by, or by certain members of, a Local Committee is not made before such date as the Area Health Authority in question may determine for that appointment, the appointment shall be made by that Authority, to the exclusion of the Committee or members in question.

(3) A Local Committee—

(a) the members of which are mentioned in paragraphs (f) and (g) of sub-paragraph (1) may, if they think fit, appoint, in addition to the member of the Family Practitioner Committee appointed by them, an ophthalmic or, as the case may be, a dispensing optician to be the deputy of the member so appointed ; and

(b) by which such a practitioner as is mentioned in paragraph (c) of that sub-paragraph is appointed in pursuance of that paragraph as a member of a Family Practitioner Committee may if it thinks fit appoint another practitioner to be his deputy.

A deputy appointed in pursuance of this sub-paragraph may, while the member for whom he is deputy is absent from any meeting of the relevant Family Practitioner Committee, act as a member of that Committee in the place of the absent member.

7.—(1) If it appears to the Secretary of State that, by reason of special circumstances affecting the area of an Area Health Authority, it is appropriate that the Family Practitioner Committee established by the Authority should not be in accordance with paragraph 6 above, he may by order provide that that paragraph shall apply in relation to the Committee with such modifications as are specified in the order.

(2) It is the Secretary of State's duty—

    (a) before he makes an order under sub-paragraph (1) above in respect of any Family Practitioner Committee, to consult that Committee with respect to the order ; and

    (b) in making any such order, to have regard to the desirability of maintaining, so far as practicable, the same numerical proportion as between members falling to be appointed by different bodies in pursuance of paragraph 6 apart from any modification.

## PART III

### SUPPLEMENTARY PROVISIONS

#### *Corporate status*

8. Each Regional Health Authority, Area Health Authority, special health authority and Family Practitioner Committee (hereinafter in this Schedule referred to severally as " an authority ") shall be a body corporate.

#### *Pay and allowances*

9.—(1) The Secretary of State may pay to the chairman of an authority other than a Family Practitioner Committee such remuneration as he may determine with the approval of the Minister for the Civil Service.

(2) The Secretary of State may provide as he may determine with the approval of the Minister for the Civil Service for the payment of a pension, allowance or gratuity to or in respect of the chairman of an authority other than such a Committee.

(3) Where a person ceases to be chairman of an authority other than such a Committee, and it appears to the Secretary of State that there are special circumstances which make it right for that person to receive compensation, the Secretary of State may make to him a payment of such amount as the Secretary of State may determine with the approval of the Minister for the Civil Service.

(4) The Secretary of State may pay to a member of an authority, or of a committee or sub-committee of an authority, such travelling

and other allowances (including attendance allowance or compensation for the loss of remunerative time) as he may determine with the approval of the Minister for the Civil Service.

(5) Allowances shall not be paid in pursuance of sub-paragraph (4) above except in connection with the exercise, in such circumstances as the Secretary of State may determine with the approval of the Minister for the Civil Service, of such functions as he may so determine.

(6) Payments under this paragraph shall be made at such times, and in such manner and subject to such conditions, as the Secretary of State may determine with the approval of the Minister for the Civil Service.

*Staff*

10.—(1) An authority other than a Family Practitioner Committee may employ, on such terms as it may determine in accordance with regulations and such directions as may be given by the Secretary of State, such officers as it may so determine ; and regulations made for the purposes of this sub-paragraph may contain provision—

(a) with respect to the qualifications of persons who may be employed as officers of an authority ;

(b) requiring an authority to employ, for the purpose of performing prescribed functions of the authority or any other body, officers having prescribed qualifications or experience ; and

(c) as to the manner in which any officers of an authority are to be appointed.

(2) Regulations may provide for the transfer of officers from one authority to another which is not a Family Practitioner Committee, and for arrangements under which the services of an officer of an authority are placed at the disposal of another authority or a local authority.

(3) Directions may be given—

(a) by the Secretary of State to an authority to place services of any of its officers at the disposal of another authority,

(b) subject to any directions given by the Secretary of State in pursuance of this sub-paragraph, by a Regional Health Authority to an Area Health Authority of which the area is included in its region to place services of any of its officers at the disposal of another such Area Health Authority,

(c) by the Secretary of State to any authority other than a Family Practitioner Committee to employ as an officer of the authority any person who is or was employed by another authority and is specified in the direction,

(d) by a Regional Health Authority to an Area Health Authority of which the area is included in its region to employ as an officer of the Area Health Authority any person who is or was employed by an authority other than the Area Health Authority and is specified in the direction, and it shall be the duty of an authority to which directions are given in pursuance of this sub-paragraph to comply with the directions.

(4) Regulations made in pursuance of this paragraph shall not require that all consultants employed by an authority are to be so employed whole-time.

11.—(1) It shall be the duty of the Secretary of State, before he makes regulations in pursuance of paragraph 10 above, to consult such bodies as he may recognise as representing persons who, in his opinion, are likely to be affected by the regulations.

(2) Subject to sub-paragraph (3) below, it is the Secretary of State's duty, or, as the case may be, a Regional Health Authority's, before he or the Authority gives directions to an authority in pursuance of sub-paragraph (3) of paragraph 10 above in respect of any officer of an authority—

(a) to consult the officer about the directions ; or

(b) to satisfy himself or itself that the authority of which he is an officer has consulted the officer about the placing or employment in question ; or

(c) to consult, except in the case of a direction in pursuance of paragraph (c) or paragraph (d) of paragraph 10(3), with respect to the directions such body as he or the Authority may recognise as representing the officer.

(3) If the Secretary of State or Regional Health Authority—

(a) considers it necessary to give directions in pursuance of paragraph (a) or paragraph (b) of paragraph 10(3) for the purpose of dealing temporarily with an emergency, and

(b) has previously consulted bodies recognised by him or the Authority as representing the relevant officers about the giving of directions for that purpose,

the Secretary of State or the Authority shall be entitled to disregard sub-paragraph (2) above in relation to the directions.

### *Miscellaneous*

12. Provision may be made by regulations as to—

(a) the appointment and tenure of office of the chairman and members of an authority ;

(b) the appointment of, and the exercise of functions by, committees and sub-committees of an authority (including joint committees and joint sub-committees of two or more authorities, and committees and sub-committees consisting wholly or partly of persons who are not members of the authority in question) ; and

(c) the procedure of an authority, and of such committees and sub-committees as are mentioned in sub-paragraph (b) above.

13. An authority may pay subscriptions, of such amounts as the Secretary of State may approve, to the funds of such bodies as he may approve.

14. The proceedings of an authority shall not be invalidated by any vacancy in its membership, or by any defect in a member's appointment.

15.—(1) An authority shall, notwithstanding that it is exercising any function on behalf of the Secretary of State or another authority, be entitled to enforce any rights acquired in the exercise of that function, and be liable in respect of any liabilities incurred (including liabilities in tort) in the exercise of that function, in all respects as if it were acting as a principal.

Proceedings for the enforcement of such rights and liabilities shall be brought, and brought only, by or, as the case may be, against the authority in question in its own name.

(2) An authority shall not be entitled to claim in any proceedings any privilege of the Crown in respect of the discovery or production of documents.

This sub-paragraph shall not prejudice any right of the Crown to withhold or procure the withholding from production of any document on the ground that its disclosure would be contrary to the public interest.

(3) The Secretary of State may by order provide—

(*a*) that any right which a Regional Hospital Board, a Board of Governors or a Hospital Management Committee was entitled to enforce by virtue of section 13 of the National Health Service Act 1946 immediately before 1st April 1974, and

(*b*) that any liability in respect of which such a board or committee was liable by virtue of that section immediately before that day,

1946 c. 81.

shall, on and after that day, be enforceable by or, as the case may be, against a health authority specified in the order as if the health authority so specified were concerned as a principal with the matter in question and did not exercise functions on behalf of the Secretary of State.

A statutory instrument containing only an order made by virtue of this sub-paragraph shall be laid before Parliament after being made.

16. Provision may be made by regulations with respect to the recording of information by an authority, and the furnishing of information by an authority to the Secretary of State or another authority.

# SCHEDULE 6

## ADDITIONAL PROVISIONS AS TO LOCAL ADVISORY COMMITTEES

1.—(1) Where the Secretary of State is satisfied that a committee formed for Wales, or for the region of a Regional Health Authority, or the area of an Area Health Authority, is representative of—

(*a*) any category of persons (other than a category mentioned in section 19(1) above) who provide services forming part of the health service, or (*b*) two or more of any of the categories mentioned in that sub-section and paragraph (*a*) above,

and that it is in the interests of the health service to recognise the committee, it shall be his duty to recognise it in pursuance of this sub-paragraph, and to determine that it shall be known by a name specified in the determination.

(2) Where a committee recognised in pursuance of sub-paragraph (1) above appears to the Secretary of State to represent categories of persons which include a category mentioned in section 19(1), he shall not be required by virtue of that subsection to recognise a committee representing persons of that category.

2. The Secretary of State may, by notice in writing served on any member of a duly recognised committee, withdraw his recognition of the committee if he considers it expedient to do so—

   (*a*) where the committee is recognised in pursuance of section 19(1) or (3) above or paragraph 1(1)(*a*) above, with a view to recognising in pursuance of paragraph 1(1)(*b*) another committee representing categories of persons which include the category represented by the recognised committee ; or

   (*b*) where the committee is recognised in pursuance of paragraph 1(1)(*b*), with a view to recognising in pursuance of any of the provisions of section 19 and paragraph 1 other committees which together are representative of the categories in question.

3. It is the duty of any duly recognised committee for Wales—

   (*a*) to advise the Secretary of State on the provision by him of services of a kind provided by the categories of persons of whom the committee is representative, and

   (*b*) to perform such other functions as may be prescribed,

4. It is the duty of a committee duly recognised by reference to the region of a Regional Health Authority or the area of an Area Health Authority—

   (*a*) to advise the Authority on the Authority's provision of services of a kind provided by the categories of persons of whom the committee is representative, and

   (*b*) to perform such other functions as may be prescribed,

and it shall be the duty of the Authority to consult the committee with respect to such matters, and on such occasions, as may be prescribed.

5. An Authority may defray such expenses incurred by a committee in performing the duty imposed on the committee by paragraphs 3 or 4 above as the Authority considers reasonable, and those expenses may include travelling and other allowances and compensation for loss of remunerative time at such rates as the Secretary of State may determine with the approval of the Minister for the Civil Service.

In this paragraph " an Authority " means—

   (*a*) in relation to any duly recognised committee for Wales, the Secretary of State ;

(b) in relation to the region of a Regional Health Authority, that Regional Health Authority ;

(c) in relation to the area of an Area Health Authority, that Area Health Authority.

SCHEDULE 7

ADDITIONAL PROVISIONS AS TO COMMUNITY HEALTH COUNCILS

1. It is the duty of a Community Health Council (in this Schedule referred to as a " Council ")—

(a) to represent the interests in the health service of the public in its district ; and

(b) to perform such other functions as may be conferred on it by virtue of paragraph 2 below.

2. Regulations may provide as to—

(a) the membership of Councils (including the election by members of a Council of a chairman of the Council) ;

(b) the proceedings of Councils ;

(c) the staff, premises and expenses of Councils ;

(d) the consultation of Councils by Area Health Authorities with respect to such matters, and on such occasions, as may be prescribed ;

(e) the furnishing of information to Councils by Area Health Authorities, and the rights of members of Councils to enter and inspect premises controlled by Area Health Authorities ;

(f) the consideration by Councils of matters relating to the operation of the health service within their districts, and the giving of advice by Councils to Area Health Authorities on such matters ;

(g) the preparation and publication of reports by Councils on such matters, and the furnishing and publication by Area Health Authorities of comments on the reports ; and

(h) the functions to be exercised by Councils in addition to the functions exercisable by them by virtue of paragraph 1(a) above and the preceding provisions of this paragraph.

3. It is the Secretary of State's duty to exercise his power to make regulations in pursuance of paragraph 2(a) above so as to secure as respects each Council that—

(a) at least one member of the Council is appointed by each local authority of which the area or part of it is included in the Council's district, and at least half of the members of the Council consist of persons appointed by those local authorities ;

(b) at least one third of the members are appointed in a prescribed manner by bodies (other than public or local authorities) of which the activities are carried on otherwise than for profit ;

(c) the other members of the Council are appointed by such bodies, and in such manner and after such consultations as may be prescribed ; and

(d) no member of the Council is also a member of a Regional Health Authority or Area Health Authority.

4. Nothing in paragraph 3 above affects the validity of anything done by or in relation to a Council during any period during which, by reason of a vacancy in the membership of the Council or a defect in the appointment of a member of it, a requirement included in regulations in pursuance of that paragraph is not satisfied.

5. The Secretary of State may by regulations—

(a) provide for the establishment of a body—

(i) to advise Councils with respect to the performance of their functions, and to assist Councils in the performance of their functions ; and

(ii) to perform such other functions as may be prescribed ; and

(b) provide for the membership, proceedings, staff, premises and expenses of that body.

6. The Secretary of State may pay to members of Councils and any body established under paragraph 5 above such travelling and other allowances (including compensation for loss of remunerative time) as he may determine with the consent of the Minister for the Civil Service.

7. In this Schedule—

" local authority " means the council of a London borough, or of a county or district as defined in relation to England in section 270(1) of the Local Government Act 1972, or of 1972 c. 70. a county or district mentioned in section 20(3) of that Act (which relates to Wales) or the Common Council of the City of London, and

" district ", in relation to a Council, means the locality for which it is established, whether that locality consists of the area or part of the area of an Area Health Authority, or such an area or part together with the areas or parts of the areas of other Area Health Authorities,

and the district of a Council must be such that no part of it is separated from the rest of it by territory not included in the district.

# SCHEDULE 8

Section 21.

## LOCAL SOCIAL SERVICES AUTHORITIES

### *Care of mothers and young children*

1.—(1) A local social services authority may, with the Secretary of State's approval, and to such extent as he may direct shall, make arrangements for the care of expectant and nursing mothers and of children who have not attained the age of 5 years and are not attending primary schools maintained by a local education authority.

(2) A local social services authority may make and recover from persons availing themselves of the services provided under this paragraph such charges (if any) in respect of residential accommodation, day nurseries, child-minders, food or articles provided as the authority consider reasonable, having regard to the means of those persons.

### *Prevention, care and after-care*

2.—(1) A local social services authority may, with the Secretary of State's approval, and to such extent as he may direct shall, make arrangements for the purpose of the prevention of illness and for the care of persons suffering from illness and for the after-care of persons who have been so suffering and in particular for—

> (a) the provision, equipment and maintenance of residential accommodation for the care of persons with a view to preventing them from becoming ill, the care of persons suffering from illness and the after-care of persons who have been so suffering ;
>
> (b) the provision, for persons whose care is undertaken with a view to preventing them from becoming ill, persons suffering from illness and persons who have been so suffering, of centres or other facilities for training them or keeping them suitably occupied and the equipment and maintenance of such centres ;
>
> (c) the provision, for the benefit of such persons as are mentioned in paragraph (b) above, of ancillary or supplemental services ; and
>
> (d) as regards persons suffering from mental disorder within the meaning of the Mental Health Act 1959, the appointment of officers to act as mental welfare officers under that Act and, in the case of such persons so suffering as are received into guardianship under Part IV of that Act (whether the guardianship of the local social services authority or of other persons), the exercise of the functions of the authority in respect of them.

Such an authority shall neither have the power nor be subject to a duty to make under this paragraph arrangements to provide facilities for any of the purposes mentioned in section 15(1) of the Disabled Persons (Employment) Act 1944.

(2) No arrangements under this paragraph shall provide for the payment of money to persons for whose benefit they are made except—

> (a) in so far as they may provide for the remuneration of such persons engaged in suitable work in accordance with the arrangements ; or
>
> (b) to persons who—
>> (i) are, or have been, suffering from mental disorder within the meaning of the Mental Health Act 1959,
>>
>> (ii) are under the age of 16 years, and
>>
>> (iii) are resident in accommodation provided under the arrangements,

of such amounts as the local social services authority think fit in respect of their occasional personal expenses where it appears to that authority that no such payment would otherwise be made.

(3) The Secretary of State may make regulations as to the conduct of premises in which, in pursuance of arrangements made under this paragraph, are provided for persons whose care is undertaken with a view to preventing them from becoming sufferers from mental disorder within the meaning of that Act of 1959 or who are, or have been, so suffering, residential accommodation or facilities for training them or keeping them suitably occupied.

(4) Any such regulations may in particular confer on the Secretary of State's officers so authorised such powers of inspection as may be prescribed by the regulations.

(5) A local social services authority may recover from persons availing themselves of services provided in pursuance of arrangements under this paragraph such charges (if any) as the authority consider reasonable, having regard to the means of those persons.

### *Home help and laundry facilities*

3.—(1) It is the duty of every local social services authority to provide on such a scale as is adequate for the needs of their area, or to arrange for the provision on such a scale as is so adequate, of home help for households where such help is required owing to the presence of—

(*a*) a person who is suffering from illness, lying-in, an expectant mother, aged, handicapped as a result of having suffered from illness or by congenital deformity, or

(*b*) a child who has not attained the age which, for the purposes of the Education Act 1944 is, in his case, the upper limit 1944 c. 31. of the compulsory school age,

and every such authority has power to provide or arrange for the provision of laundry facilities for households for which home help is being, or can be, provided under this sub-paragraph.

(2) A local social services authority may recover from persons availing themselves of help or faciilties provided under this paragraph such charges (if any) as the authority consider reasonable, having regard to the means of those persons.

## SCHEDULE 9                    Section 46.

### Tribunal for Purposes of Section 46

### *Constitution of Tribunal*

1. The Tribunal shall consist of a chairman and two other members.

2. The chairman shall be a practising barrister or solicitor of not less than ten years' standing appointed by the Lord Chancellor.

3. One of the other members shall be a person appointed by the Secretary of State after consultation with such associations of Family Practitioner Committees as the Secretary of State may recognise as representative of Family Practitioner Committees.

4. The remaining member (referred to in paragraph 5 below as "the practitioner member") shall be appointed by the Secretary of State from such one of the panels appointed as provided below as the Secretary of State considers appropriate having regard to the profession or calling of the person whose case is to be investigated.

For the purposes of this paragraph, the Secretary of State shall, after consultations with such organisations as he may recognise as representative of the several professions or callings concerned, appoint the following panels, none of which shall exceed six persons—

    (*a*) a panel of medical practitioners,

    (*b*) a panel of medical practitioners having the qualifications prescribed under section 38 above,

    (*c*) a panel of dental practitioners,

    (*d*) a panel of ophthalmic opticians,

    (*e*) a panel of dispensing opticians,

    (*f*) a panel of registered pharmacists.

5. If any member of the Tribunal is unable to act in any case, a deputy may be appointed by the Lord Chancellor or the Secretary of State as in the case of the appointment of the member in question.

If the member is the chairman, the deputy shall possess the professional qualifications required for the office of chairman, and, if the member is the practitioner member, the deputy shall be appointed from the same panel.

### *Supplementary*

6. Regulations may provide for the appointment, tenure of office and vacation of office of members of the Tribunal, and with respect to the appointment of officers of the Tribunal.

# SCHEDULE 10

### ADDITIONAL PROVISIONS AS TO PROHIBITION OF SALE OF MEDICAL PRACTICES

### *Prohibition, and certificate of Medical Practices Committee*

1.—(1) Any person who sells or buys the goodwill, or any part of the goodwill, of a medical practice which it is unlawful to sell by virtue of section 54(1) above is guilty of an offence and liable on conviction on indictment to a fine not exceeding—

    (*a*) such amount as will in the court's opinion secure that he derives no benefit from the offence, and

(*b*) the further amount of £500,
or to imprisonment for a term not exceeding three months, or to
both such fine and such imprisonment.

(2) Any medical practitioner or his personal representative may
apply to the Medical Practices Committee for their opinion whether
a proposed transaction or series of transactions involves the sale of
the goodwill, or any part of the goodwill, of a medical practice
which it is unlawful to sell by virtue of section 54(1).

(3) The Committee shall consider any such application, and, if
they are satisfied that the transaction or series of transactions does
not involve the giving of valuable consideration in respect of the
goodwill, or any part of the goodwill, of such a medical practice,
they shall issue to the applicant a certificate to that effect, which
shall be in the prescribed form and shall set out all material circumstances disclosed to the Committee.

(4) Where any person is charged with an offence under this paragraph in respect of any transaction or series of transactions, it shall
be a defence to the charge to prove that the transaction or series of
transactions was certified by the Medical Practices Committee under
sub-paragraph (3) above.

(5) Any document purporting to be such a certificate shall be
admissible in evidence and shall be deemed to be such a certificate
unless the contrary is proved.

(6) If it appears to the court that the applicant for any such
certificate failed to disclose to the Committee all the material circumstances, or made any misrepresentation with respect thereto,
the court may disregard the certificate, and sub-paragraph (4) shall
not apply thereto.

(7) A prosecution for an offence under this paragraph shall only
be instituted by or with the consent of the Director of Public Pro-
secutions, and the Medical Practices Committee shall, at the request
of the Director, furnish him with a copy of any certificate issued by
them under sub-paragraph (3), and with copies of any documents
produced to them in connection with the application for that certificate.

(8) For the purposes of this paragraph (and paragraph 2 below)
references to the goodwill of a medical practice shall, in relation to
a medical practitioner practising in partnership, be construed as
referring to his share of the goodwill of the partnership practice.

*Certain transactions deemed sale of goodwill*

2.—(1) Where—
   (*a*) any medical practitioner or his personal representative
        knowingly sells or lets premises previously used by that
        practitioner for the purposes of his practice to another
        medical practitioner, or in any other way disposes or
        procures the disposition of the premises whether by a single

transaction or a series of transactions, with a view to enabling another practitioner to use the premises for the purposes of his practice, and

(*b*) the consideration for the sale, letting or other disposition is substantially in excess of the consideration which might reasonably have been expected if the premises had not previously been used for the purposes of a medical practice,

the sale, letting or other disposition of the premises shall be deemed for the purposes of section 54(1) and paragraph 1 above to be a sale by the first medical practitioner or his personal representative of the goodwill, or part of the goodwill, of the practice of that practitioner to that other practitioner.

Where a medical practitioner or his personal representative sells, lets or disposes or procures the disposition, of any premises, together with any other property, the court shall, for the purposes of this sub-paragraph, make such apportionment of the consideration as it thinks just.

(2) Where in pursuance of any partnership agreement between medical practitioners—

(*a*) any valuable consideration, other than the performance of services in the partnership business, is given by a partner or proposed partner as consideration for his being taken into partnership,

(*b*) any valuable consideration is given to a partner, on or in contemplation of his retirement or of his acceptance of a reduced share of the partnership profits, or to the personal representative of a partner on his death, not being a payment in respect of that partner's share in past earnings of the partnership or in any partnership assets or any other payment required to be made to him as the result of the final settlement of accounts, as between him and the other partners, in respect of past transactions of the partnership, or

(*c*) services are performed by any partner for a consideration substantially less than those services might reasonably have been expected to be worth having regard to the circumstances at the time when the agreement was made,

there shall be deemed for the purposes of section 54(1) and paragraph 1 to have been a sale of the goodwill, or part of the goodwill, of the practice of any partner to whom, or to whose personal representative, the consideration or any part thereof is given or, as the case may be, for whose benefit the services are performed, to the partner or each of the partners by or on whose behalf the consideration or any part thereof was given or, as the case may be, the partner who performed the services, and the said sale shall be deemed for the purposes of section 54(1) and paragraph 1 to have been effected—

(i) in a case to which paragraph (*a*) or paragraph (*b*) applies, at the time when the consideration was given, or, if the consideration was not all given at the same time, at the time when the first part thereof was given, or

     (ii) in a case to which paragraph (*c*) applies, at the Sᴄʜ. 10
time when the agreement was made.

(3) Where any medical practitioner—

(*a*) performs services as an assistant to another medical practitioner for remuneration substantially less than those services might reasonably have been expected to be worth having regard to the circumstances at the time when the remuneration was fixed, and

(*b*) subsequently succeeds, whether as the result of a partnership agreement or otherwise, to the practice or any part of the practice of the second practitioner,

there shall be deemed for the purposes of section 54(1) and paragraph 1 to have been a sale (effected at the time when the remuneration was fixed) of the goodwill, or part of the goodwill, of that practice by the second practitioner to the first practitioner, unless it is shown that that remuneration of the first practitioner was not fixed in contemplation of his succeeding to the practice, or any part of it.

(4) For the purposes of section 54(1) and paragraph 1—

(*a*) if a medical practitioner or the personal representative of a medical practitioner agrees, for valuable consideration, to do or refrain from doing any act, or to allow any act to be done, for the purpose of facilitating the succession of another medical practitioner to the practice, or any part of the practice, of the first practitioner, the transaction shall be deemed to be a sale of the goodwill, or part of the goodwill, of that practice by the first practitioner or his personal representative to the second practitioner ; and

(*b*) if any medical practitioner, or any person acting on his behalf, gives any valuable consideration to another medical practitioner, or the personal representative of another medical practitioner, and the first medical practitioner succeeds, or has succeeded, whether before or after the transaction aforesaid, to the practice, or any part of the practice, of the second practitioner, the transaction shall be deemed to be a sale of the goodwill, or part of the goodwill, of the practice of the second practitioner by him or by his personal representative to the first practitioner, unless it is shown that no part of the consideration was given in respect of the said goodwill or part of it.

(5) Sub-paragraph (4) above shall not apply to anything done in relation to the acquisition of premises for the purposes of a medical practice, or in pursuance of a partnership agreement, or to the performance of services as an assistant to a medical practitioner.

(6) In determining for the purposes of section 54(1) and this Schedule the consideration given in respect of any transaction, the court shall have regard to any other transaction appearing to the court to be associated with the first transaction, and shall estimate the total consideration given in respect of both or all the transactions, and apportion it between those transactions in such manner as it thinks just.

E

SCH. 10

(7) Where any consideration is, with the knowledge and consent of a medical practitioner or his personal representative, given to any other person, and it appears to the court that the medical practitioner or, if he has died, his estate or some person beneficially interested in his estate derives a substantial benefit from the giving of the consideration, the consideration shall be deemed for the purposes of section 54(1) and this Schedule to have been given to the medical practitioner or his personal representative, as the case may be.

Section 57.

## SCHEDULE 11

### ADDITIONAL PROVISIONS AS TO THE CONTROL OF MAXIMUM PRICES FOR MEDICAL SUPPLIES

#### Orders and directions

1.—(1) Any power of making orders under section 57 above includes power to provide for any incidental and supplementary provisions which the Secretary of State thinks it expedient for the purposes of the order to provide.

(2) An order under section 57 may make such provisions (including provision for requiring any person to furnish any information) as the Secretary of State thinks necessary or expedient for facilitating the introduction or operation of a scheme of control for which provision has been made, or for which, in his opinion, it will or may be found necessary or expedient that provision should be made, under that section.

(3) An order under section 57 may prohibit the doing of anything regulated by the order except under the authority of a licence granted by such authority or person as may be specified in the order, and may be made so as to apply either to persons or undertakings generally or to any particular person or undertaking or class of persons or undertakings, and so as to have effect either generally or in any particular area.

1889 c. 63.

(4) The Interpretation Act 1889 shall apply to the interpretation of any order made under section 57 as it applies to the interpretation of an Act of Parliament and for the purposes of section 38 of that Act any such order shall be deemed to be an Act of Parliament.

#### Notices, authorisations and proof of documents

2.—(1) A notice to be served on any person for the purposes of section 57 above, or of any order or direction made or given under that section, shall be deemed to have been duly served on the person to whom it is directed if—

    (a) it is delivered to him personally ; or

    (b) it is sent by registered post or the recorded delivery service addressed to him at his last or usual place of abode or place of business.

(2) Where under section 57 and this Schedule a person has power to authorise other persons to act thereunder, the power may be exercised so as to confer the authority either on particular persons or on a specified class of persons.

(3) Any permit, licence, permission or authorisation granted for SCH. 11
the purposes of section 57 may be revoked at any time by the
authority or person empowered to grant it.

(4) Every document purporting to be an instrument made or issued
by the Secretary of State or other authority or person in pursuance
of section 57 and this Schedule or any provisions so having effect and
to be signed by or on behalf of the Secretary of State, or that
authority or person, shall be received in evidence and shall until the
contrary is proved, be deemed to be an instrument made or issued
by the Secretary of State, or that authority or person.

(5) Prima facie evidence of any such instrument as is described
in sub-paragraph (4) above may in any legal proceedings (including
arbitrations) be given by the production of a document purporting
to be certified to be a true copy of the instrument by or on behalf
of the Secretary of State or other authority or person having power
to make or issue the instrument.

### *Territorial extent*

3. So far as any provisions contained in or having effect under
section 57 above and this Schedule impose prohibitions, restrictions
or obligations on persons, those provisions apply to all persons in
the United Kingdom and all persons on board any British ship or
aircraft, not being an excepted ship or aircraft, and to all other
persons, wherever they may be, who are ordinarily resident in the
United Kingdom and who are citizens of the United Kingdom and
Colonies or British protected persons.

In this paragraph—

" British aircraft " means an aircraft registered in—

(a) any part of Her Majesty's dominions ;

(b) any country outside Her Majesty's dominions in
which for the time being Her Majesty has jurisdiction ;

(c) any country consisting partly of one or more
colonies and partly of one or more such countries as are
mentioned in paragraph (b) above ;

" British protected person " means the same as in the British
Nationality Acts 1948 to 1965 ;

" excepted ship or aircraft " means a ship or aircraft registered
in any country for the time being listed in section 1(3) of
the British Nationality Act 1948 or in any territory adminis- 1948 c. 56.
tered by the government of any such country, not being a
ship or aircraft for the time being placed at the disposal
of, or chartered by or on behalf of, Her Majesty's Government in the United Kingdom.

### *False documents and false statements*

4.—(1) A person shall not, with intent to deceive—

(a) use any document issued for the purposes of section 57
above and this Schedule or of any order made under that
section ;

(b) have in his possession any document so closely resembling such a document as is described in paragraph (a) above as to be calculated to deceive ;

(c) produce, furnish, send or otherwise make use of for purposes connected with that section and this Schedule or any order or direction made or given under that section, any book, account, estimate, return, declaration or other document which is false in a material particular.

(2) A person shall not, in furnishing any information for the purposes of section 57 and this Schedule or of any order made under that section, make a statement which he knows to be false in a material particular or recklessly make a statement which is false in a material particular.

### Restrictions on disclosing information

5. No person who obtains any information by virtue of section 57 above and this Schedule shall, otherwise than in connection with the execution of that section and this Schedule or of an order made under that section, disclose that information except for the purposes of any criminal proceedings, or of a report of any criminal proceedings, or with permission granted by or on behalf of a Minister of the Crown.

### Offences by corporations

6. Where an offence under this Schedule committed by a body corporate is proved to have been committed with the consent or connivance of, or to be attributable to any neglect on the part of, any director, manager, secretary or other similar officer of the body corporate or any person who was purporting to act in any such capacity, he, as well as the body corporate, shall be guilty of that offence and shall be liable to be proceeded against and punished accordingly.

In this paragraph, the expression " director ", in relation to a body corporate established by or under any enactment for the purpose of carrying on under national ownership any industry or part of an industry or undertaking, being a body corporate whose affairs are managed by its members, means a member of that body corporate.

### Penalties

7.—(1) If any person contravenes or fails to comply with any order made under section 57 above, or any direction given or requirement imposed under that section, or contravenes or fails to comply with this Schedule (except for paragraph 8(3) or paragraph 9(4) below) he is, save as otherwise expressly provided, guilty of an offence.

(2) Subject to any special provisions contained in this Schedule, a person guilty of such an offence shall—

(a) on summary conviction, be liable to imprisonment for a term not exceeding three months or to a fine not exceeding £100, or to both ; or

(*b*) on conviction on indictment, be liable to imprisonment for    
a term not exceeding two years or to a fine not exceeding
£500, or to both.

(3) Where a person convicted on indictment of such an offence
is a body corporate, no provision limiting the amount of the fine
which may be imposed shall apply, and the body corporate shall be
liable to a fine of such amount as the court thinks just.

### Production of documents

8.—(1) For the purposes—
  (*a*) of securing compliance with any order made or direction
       given under section 57 above by or on behalf of the
       Secretary of State, or
  (*b*) of verifying any estimates, returns or information furnished
       to the Secretary of State in connection with section 57 or
       any order made or direction given under that section,

an officer of the Secretary of State duly authorised in that behalf has
power, on producing (if required to do so) evidence of his authority,
to require any person carrying on an undertaking or employed in
connection with an undertaking to produce to that officer forthwith
any documents relating to the undertaking which that officer may
reasonably require for the purpose set out above.

(2) The power conferred by this paragraph to require any person
to produce documents includes power—
  (*a*) if the documents are produced, to take copies of them or
       extracts from them and to require that person, or where
       that person is a body corporate, any other person who is
       a present or past officer of, or is employed by, the body
       corporate, to provide an explanation of any of them ;
  (*b*) if the documents are not produced, to require the person
       who was required to produce them to state, to the best of
       his knowledge and belief, where they are.

(3) If any requirement to produce documents or provide an
explanation or make a statement which is imposed by virtue of this
paragraph is not complied with, the person on whom the requirement
was so imposed is guilty of an offence and liable on summary conviction to imprisonment for a term not exceeding three months or to
a fine not exceeding £100, or to both.

Where a person is charged with such an offence in respect of a
requirement to produce any document, it shall be a defence to prove
that they were not in his possession or under his control and that
it was not reasonably practicable for him to comply with the
requirements.

9.—(1) If a justice of the peace is satisfied, on information on oath
laid on the Secretary of State's behalf, that there are any reasonable grounds for suspecting that there are on any premises any
documents of which production has been required by virtue of
paragraph 8 above and which have not been produced in compliance
with that requirement, he may issue a warrant under this paragraph.

E 3

A warrant so issued may authorise any constable, together with any other persons named in the warrant and any other constables—

    (*a*) to enter the premises specified in the information (using such force as is reasonably necessary for the purpose) ; and

    (*b*) to search the premises and take possession of any documents appearing to be such documents as are mentioned above, or to take in relation to any documents so appearing any other steps which may appear necessary for preserving them and preventing interference with them.

(2) Every warrant issued under this paragraph shall continue in force until the end of the period of one month after the date on which it is issued.

(3) Any documents of which possession is taken under this paragraph may be retained for a period of three months or, if within that period there are commenced any proceedings for an offence under section 57 above and this Schedule to which they are relevant, until the conclusion of those proceedings.

(4) Any person who obstructs the exercise of any right of entry or search conferred by virtue of a warrant under this paragraph, or who obstructs the exercise of any rights so conferred to take possession of any documents, is guilty of an offence and liable on summary conviction to imprisonment for a term not exceeding three months or to a fine not exceeding £50, or to both.

### *Northern Ireland*

10.—(1) So far as the Secretary of State's power under section 57 above and this Schedule is exercisable in relation to Northern Ireland—

    (*a*) he may, to such extent and subject to such restrictions as he thinks proper, by order delegate that power either to a Northern Ireland department or departments specified in that order or to the appropriate Northern Ireland department or departments ; and

    (*b*) where any power is so delegated to the appropriate Northern Ireland department or departments, that power shall be exercised by such Northern Ireland department or departments as the Secretary of State may by order specify.

(2) The power of the Secretary of State to make an order under sub-paragraph (1)(*b*) above shall be exercisable by statutory instrument ; and where a power to make orders has been delegated in pursuance of sub-paragraph (1)—

    (*a*) any order made in pursuance of that power shall be made by statutory instrument ; and

1946 c. 36.     (*b*) the Statutory Instruments Act 1946 shall apply in like manner as if the order had been made by the Secretary of State.

(3) The references in section 57(1) and (2) above to this Act include any corresponding enactments of the Parliament of Northern Ireland or the Northern Ireland Assembly.

## SCHEDULE 12

ADDITIONAL PROVISIONS AS TO REGULATIONS FOR THE
MAKING AND RECOVERY OF CHARGES

*Regulations under section 77—charges for drugs, medicines or
appliances, or pharmaceutical services*

1.—(1) No charge shall be made under section 77(1) above in
relation to the supply of drugs, medicines and appliances referred to
in paragraph (*a*) of that subsection in respect of—

(*a*) the supply of any drug, medicine or appliance for a patient
who is for the time being resident in hospital, or

(*b*) the supply of any drug or medicine for the treatment of
venereal disease, or

(*c*) the supply of any appliance (otherwise than in pursuance of
paragraph (*b*) of section 5(1) above) for a person who is
under 16 years of age or is undergoing full-time education
in a school, or

(*d*) the replacement or repair of any appliance in consequence
of a defect in the appliance as supplied,

and regulations may provide for the remission or repayment of any
charge payable under paragraph (*a*) of section 77(1) in such other
cases as may be prescibed.

(2) Regulations made under section 77(1) above in relation to
the pharmaceutical services referred to in paragraph (*b*) of that
subsection may provide for the remission or repayment of the
charges made by those regulations in the case of such persons as
may be prescribed.

*Regulations under section 78—charges for dental or
optical appliances*

2.—(1) The dental and optical appliances mentioned in the first
column below, and the charges mentioned in the second column, are
the appliances and charges referred to in section 78(1) above.

| *Appliance* | *Charge* |
|---|---|
| The dentures described in regulations made under section 78(1) and this paragraph. | The amount or the maximum amount prescribed by regulations made under section 78(1) and this paragraph. |
| Glasses other than children's glasses—<br>   The lenses described in regulations made under section 78(1) and this paragraph. | The amount or the maximum amount prescribed by regulations made under section 78(1) and this paragraph. |
| Frames. | The current specified cost. |

In this sub-paragraph—

" children's glasses " means glasses for which a standard type
of children's frame as described in the Statement referred

SCH. 12

to below is used and which are supplied for a person who was, at the time of the examination or testing of sight leading to the supply of the glasses or of the first such examination or testing, under 16 years of age or receiving full-time education in a school, and

" current specified cost ", in relation to frames supplied under Part II of this Act, means the sum specified in the Statement as the sum payable for frames of that description by the person to whom they are supplied, and in relation to frames supplied under this Act otherwise than under Part II means a sum equal to the sum so specified, or in the case of frames of a description for which no sum is so specified, such sum as may be determined by or in accordance with directions given by the Secretary of State,

and for the purposes of this provision " the Statement " means the Statement published by the Secretary of State pursuant to the provisions of regulation 10 of the National Health Service (General Ophthalmic Services) Regulations 1974 or any corresponding regulation for the time being in force.

S.I. 1974/287.

(2) Regulations may—

(a) vary the amount or maximum amount of any charge authorised by section 78(1) for any dental or optical appliance, and this power includes power to direct that the charge shall not be payable ; or

(b) vary the descriptions of appliances for which any such charge is authorised ;

and regulations made for the purposes of section 78(1) may be made so as to take effect—

(i) in the case of appliances supplied under this Act otherwise than under Part II, where the examination or testing of sight (otherwise than under that Part) leading to the supply of those appliances, or the first such examination or testing, takes place on or after the date on which the regulations come into force ;

(ii) in the case of dental appliances supplied under Part II, where the contract or arrangement between the person by whom and the person to whom the appliances are supplied is made on or after that date ;

(iii) in the case of optical appliances supplied under Part II, where the testing of sight leading to the supply of those appliances, or the first such testing, takes place on or after that date.

(3) No charge shall be made under section 78(1) in respect of any appliance supplied otherwise than under Part II to a patient for the time being resident in a hospital.

(4) No charge shall be made under section 78(1) in respect of the supply of a dental appliance if at the relevant time the person for whom that appliance was supplied—

(a) was under 16 years of age or was receiving full-time education in a school ; or (*b*) was an expectant mother or had borne a child within the previous twelve months.

(5) No charge shall be made under section 78(1) for the supply under this Act of lenses for any glasses if—

(*a*) the person for whom the glasses are supplied was at the relevant time of the age of 10 or more and either under the age of 16 or receiving full-time education in a school ; and

(*b*) the frames of the glasses are of any description specified in the Statement referred to in sub-paragraph (1) above, or any corresponding regulation for the time being in force.

(6) Regulations made with respect to any exemption under sub-paragraph (4) or sub-paragraph (5) above may provide that it shall be a condition of the exemption that such declaration is made in such form and manner, or such certificate or other evidence is supplied in such form and manner, as may be prescribed.

(7) In sub-paragraphs (4) and (5), " the relevant time " means—

(*a*) in relation to a dental appliance supplied otherwise than under Part II, or to an optical appliance supplied under this Act, the time of the examination or testing of sight leading to the supply of the appliance, or the first such examination or testing ;

(*b*) in relation to a dental appliance supplied under Part II, the time of the making of the contract or arrangement in pursuance of which the appliance is supplied.

(8) References in section 78 and in this paragraph to the supply of appliances shall be construed as including references to their replacement, but no charge shall be made under those provisions in respect of the replacement of dentures or lenses if the replacement is required in consequence of loss or damage.

### *Regulations under section 79—charges for dental treatment*

3.—(1) The amount of the charge payable under section 79(1) above in respect of services provided in pursuance of any contract or arrangement shall be (subject to sub-paragraph (3) below) the current authorised fee for all services so provided in respect of which a charge is payable under that section or a prescribed sum, whichever is the less.

In this sub-paragraph " current authorised fee ", in relation to any services, means the fee authorised in accordance with regulations for the time being in force under this Act as the fee payable to the practitioner in respect of those services, but does not include—

(*a*) any fee so authorised in respect of a visit to a patient by a practitioner ; or

(*b*) any fee or part of a fee payable by the patient in pursuance of regulations under—

(i) section 79(2) above ;

(ii) section 81 above, in relation to paragraph (*b*) of that section ;

(iii) section 82 above, in relation to paragraph (*b*) of that section.

(2) Regulations may vary the amount or the maximum amount of any charge (including power to direct that the charge shall not be payable) authorised by section 79(1); and no charge shall be made under that section for any services provided in pursuance of a contract or arrangement under which the first examination took place before 29th May 1952.

(3) Where any services in respect of which a charge is payable under section 78 above are provided in pursuance of a contract or arrangement, the charges payable under that section and section 79(1) in respect of all services provided in pursuance of the contract or arrangement shall not exceed a prescribed sum in the aggregate.

(4) No charge shall be made under section 79(1) in respect of services provided for any person who, on the date of the contract or arrangement for the services—

    (*a*) was under 21 years of age (other than for services in respect of the relining of a denture or the addition of teeth, bands or wires to a denture),

    (*b*) was under 16 years of age or was receiving full-time education in a school,

    (*c*) was an expectant mother or had borne a child within the previous 12 months,

if (in any such case) a declaration to that effect is made by or on behalf of that person in such form and manner as may be prescribed.

(5) Regulations under section 79(1), in relation to—

    (*a*) the persons described in paragraphs (*b*) and (*c*) of sub-paragraph (4) above, and

    (*b*) any exemption in respect of the relining of a denture or the addition of teeth, bands or wires to a denture,

may provide that it shall be a condition of the exemption that such declaration is made in such form and manner, or such certificate or other evidence is supplied in such form and manner, as may be prescribed.

### Miscellaneous Provisions

4. For the purposes of paragraph (*a*) of section 5(1) above and paragraph 1(*a*) of Schedule 1 to this Act (which provide for the Secretary of State to arrange for the free medical treatment of certain pupils) any charge made in pursuance of regulations under this Act in respect of the supply of drugs, medicines or appliances shall be disregarded.

5. Regulations may provide for the remission or repayment of any charges which, in pursuance of section 78(1) above or section 79(1) above, are payable apart from this paragraph by a person whose income as calculated in accordance with regulations is at less than the prescribed rate, in respect of the supply or replacement of dental or optical appliances or in respect of services provided as part of the general dental services.

6. For the purposes of sections 77 and 78 above and of this
Schedule, a bridge, whether fixed or removable, which takes the place
of any teeth shall be deemed to be a denture having that number of
teeth ; and the reference in paragraph (*a*) of section 79(1) to appliances described in paragraph 2(1) of this Schedule shall be construed
accordingly.

Sch. 12

7. References in this Schedule to full-time education in a school
mean full-time instruction in a school within the meaning of the
Education Act 1944 or the Education (Scotland) Act 1962.

1944 c. 31.<br>1962 c. 47.

## SCHEDULE 13

ADDITIONAL PROVISIONS AS TO THE HEALTH SERVICE COMMISSIONER
FOR ENGLAND AND THE HEALTH SERVICE COMMISSIONER FOR
WALES.

Sections 114(2)<br>and 116(2).

### PART I

### PROCEDURAL AND OTHER PROVISIONS

*Procedure in respect of investigations*

1. Where the Commissioner proposes to conduct an investigation
pursuant to a complaint under Part V of this Act, he shall afford to
the relevant body concerned, and to any other person who is alleged
in the complaint to have taken or authorised the action complained
of, an opportunity to comment on any allegations contained in the
complaint.

2. Every such investigation shall be conducted in private, but
except for that the procedure for conducting an investigation shall be
such as the Commissioner considers appropriate in the
circumstances of the case.

3. Without prejudice to the generality of paragraph 2 above, the
Commissioner may obtain information from such persons and in
such manner, and make such inquiries, as he thinks fit, and may
determine whether any person may be represented, by counsel or
solicitor or otherwise, in the investigation.

4. The Commissioner may, if he thinks fit, pay to the person
by whom the complaint was made and to any other person who
attends or furnishes information for the purposes of an investigation
under Part V of this Act—

(*a*) sums in respect of expenses properly incurred by them,

(*b*) allowances by way of compensation for the loss of their
    time,

in accordance with such scales and subject to such conditions as
may be determined by the Minister for the Civil Service.

5. The conduct of an investigation under Part V of this Act
shall not affect any action taken by the relevant body concerned,
or any power or duty of that body to take further action with
respect to any matters subject to the investigation.

6. Where the person aggrieved has been removed from the United Kingdom under any Order in force under the Immigration Act 1971 he shall, if the Commissioner so directs, be permitted to re-enter and remain in the United Kingdom, subject to such conditions as the Secretary of State may direct, for the purposes of the investigation.

### Evidence

7. For the purposes of an investigation under Part V of this Act the Commissioner may require any employee, officer or member of the relevant body concerned or any other person who in his opinion is able to furnish information or produce documents relevant to the investigation to furnish any such information or produce any such document.

8. For the purposes of any such investigation the Commissioner shall have the same powers as the Court (which in this Schedule means, in relation to England and Wales, the High Court, in relation to Scotland, the Court of Session, and in relation to Northern Ireland, the High Court of Northern Ireland) in respect of the attendance and examination of witnesses (including the administration of oaths or affirmations and the examination of witnesses abroad) and in respect of the production of documents.

9. No obligation to maintain secrecy or other restriction upon the disclosure of information obtained by or furnished to persons in Her Majesty's service, whether imposed by any enactment or by any rule of law, shall apply to the disclosure of information for the purposes of an investigation under Part V of this Act.

The Crown shall not be entitled in relation to any such investigation to any such privilege in respect of the production of documents or the giving of evidence as is allowed by law in legal proceedings.

10. No person shall be required or authorised by Part V of this Act and this Schedule to furnish any information or answer any question relating to proceedings of the Cabinet or of any committee of the Cabinet or to produce so much of any document as relates to such proceedings.

For the purposes of this paragraph a certificate issued by the Secretary of the Cabinet with the approval of the Prime Minister and certifying that any information, question, document, or part of a document so relates shall be conclusive.

11. Subject to paragraph 9 above, no person shall be compelled for the purposes of an investigation under Part V of this Act to give any evidence or produce any document which he could not be compelled to give or produce in civil proceedings before the Court.

### Obstruction and contempt

12. If any person without lawful excuse obstructs the Commissioner or any officer of the Commissioner in the performance of his functions under Part V of this Act and this Schedule, or is guilty of any act or omission in relation to an investigation under that Part which,

if that investigation were a proceeding in the Court, would constitute contempt of court, the Commissioner may certify the offence to the Court.

13. Where an offence is certified under paragraph 12 above, the Court may inquire into the matter and, after hearing any witnesses who may be produced against or on behalf of the person charged with the offence, and after hearing any statement that may be offered in defence, deal with him in any manner in which the Court could deal with him if he had committed the like offence in relation to the Court.

14. Nothing in paragraphs 12 and 13 above shall be construed as applying to the taking of any such action as is mentioned in paragraphs 5 and 6 above.

### Secrecy of information

15. The Commissioner and his officers hold office under Her Majesty within the meaning of the Official Secrets Act 1911.

16. Information obtained by the Commissioner or his officers in the course of or for the purposes of an investigation under Part V of this Act shall not be disclosed except—

   (*a*) for the purposes of the investigation and of any report to be made in respect of the investigation under that Part,

   (*b*) for the purposes of any proceedings for an offence under the Official Secrets Acts 1911 to 1939 alleged to have been committed in respect of information obtained by the Commissioner or any of his officers by virtue of that Part or for an offence of perjury alleged to have been committed in the course of an investigation under that Part or for the purposes of an inquiry with a view to the taking of such proceedings, or

   (*c*) for the purposes of any proceedings under paragraphs 12 and 13 above,

and the Commissioner and his officers shall not be called upon to give evidence in any proceedings (other than those mentioned in this paragraph) of matters coming to his or their knowledge in the course of an investigation under that Part.

17. A Minister of the Crown may give notice in writing to the Commissioner, with respect to any document or information specified in the notice, or any class of documents or information so specified, that in the Minister's opinion the disclosure of that document or information, or of documents or information of that class, would be prejudicial to the safety of the State or otherwise contrary to the public interest.

18. Where a notice under paragraph 17 above is given nothing in this Schedule shall be construed as authorising or requiring the Commissioner or any officer of the Commissioner to communicate to any person or for any purpose any document or information specified in the notice, or any document or information of a class so specified.

# PART II

## *Matters not subject to investigation by the Health Service Commissioner for England or the Health Service Commissioner for Wales*

19. The following matters are not subject to investigation by the Health Service Commissioner for England or the Health Service Commissioner for Wales—

(1) Action taken in connection with the diagnosis of illness or the care or treatment of a patient, being action which, in the opinion of the Commissioner in question, was taken solely in consequence of the exercise of clinical judgment, whether formed by the person taking the action or any other person.

S.I. 1974/455.

(2) Action taken by a Family Practitioner Committee in the exercise of its functions under the National Health Service (Service Committees and Tribunal) Regulations 1974, or any instrument amending or replacing those regulations.

(3) Action taken in respect of appointments or removals, pay, discipline, superannuation or other personnel matters in relation to service under this Act.

(4) Action taken in matters relating to contractual or other commercial transactions, other than in matters arising from arrangements between a relevant body and another body which is not a relevant body for the provision of services for patients by that other body ; and in determining what matters arise from such arrangements there shall be disregarded any arrangements for the provision of services at an establishment maintained by a Minister of the Crown for patients who are mainly members of the armed forces of the Crown.

(5) Action which has been, or is, the subject of an inquiry under section 84 above.

Section 129.

# SCHEDULE 14

## TRANSITIONAL PROVISIONS AND SAVINGS

### *General*

1.—(1) In so far as—

(a) any agreement, appointment, apportionment, authorisation, determination, instrument, order or regulation made by virtue of an enactment repealed by this Act, or

(b) any approval, consent, direction, or notice given by virtue of such an enactment, or

(c) any complaint made or investigation begun by virtue of such an enactment, or

(d) any other proceedings begun by virtue of such an enactment, or

(e) anything done or having effect as if done,

could, if a corresponding enactment in this Act were in force at the relevant time, have been made, given, begun or done by virtue of the corresponding enactment, it shall, if effective immediately before the corresponding enactment comes into force, continue to have effect thereafter as if made, given. begun or done by virtue of that corresponding enactment.

    (2) Where—
>    (*a*) there is any reference in this Act (whether express or implied) to a thing done or required or authorised to be done, or to a thing omitted, or to an event which has occurred, under or for the purposes of or by reference to or in contravention of any provisions of this Act, then
>
>    (*b*) that reference shall be construed (subject to its context) as including a reference to the corresponding thing done or required or authorised to be done, or omitted, or to the corresponding event which occurred, as the case may be, under or for the purposes of or by reference to or in contravention of any of the corresponding provisions of the repealed enactments.

2. Where any instrument or document refers either expressly or by implication to an enactment repealed by this Act the reference shall (subject to its context) be construed as or as including a reference to the corresponding provision of this Act.

3. Where any period of time specified in an enactment repealed by this Act is current at the commencement of this Act, this Act has effect as if its corresponding provision had been in force when that period began to run.

### *Medical schools in London*

4. Notwithstanding the repeal by this Act of section 15 of the National Health Service Act 1946—     1946 c. 81.
>    (*a*) where a scheme was prepared and submitted under subsection (1) and approved under subsection (2) of that section, that scheme may be amended by a new scheme in accordance with subsection (3) of that section ; and
>
>    (*b*) any scheme prepared, submitted and approved under that section, or as amended under paragraph (*a*) above, shall continue to have effect, or have effect, as if that section had not been repealed.

### *Section 36 of the National Health Service Act 1946*

5. Notwithstanding the repeal by this Act of section 36 of the National Health Service Act 1946 (compensation for loss of right to sell a medical practice) that section shall continue to have such effect as may be necessary for the purposes of sections 1 to 7 of the National   1949 c. 93. Health Service (Amendment) Act 1949.

The saving made by this paragraph applies to section 51 of the National Health Service Reorganisation Act 1973 (which amended   1973 c. 32. section 36 of the National Health Service Act 1946), and to any regulations made under that section 36 which were in force immediately before the coming into force of this Act.

### *Local Acts and charters*

6.—(1) Where at the passing of the National Health Service Act 1946—
>    (*a*) there was in force a local or private Act or charter containing provisions which appear to the Secretary of State either

to be inconsistent with any of the provisions of that Act of 1946 as reproduced in this Act, or to have been made redundant in consequence of the passing of that Act of 1946, then

    (b) the Secretary of State may by order make such alterations, whether by amendment or by repeal, in the local or private Act or charter as appear to him to be necessary for the purpose of bringing its provisions into conformity with the provisions of that Act of 1946 as so reproduced, or for the purpose of removing redundant provisions, as the case may be.

(2) Any provision of a charter defining or restricting—

    (a) the objects of any hospital to which section 6 of that Act of 1946 applied, or

    (b) the purposes for which any property transferred to the Secretary of State or the Board of Governors of a teaching hospital by virtue of that Act of 1946 may be used,

shall cease to have effect.

### Persons authorised to provide pharmaceutical services

7.—(1) A person who for three years immediately before 16th December 1911 acted as a dispenser to a medical practitioner or a public institution is in the same position in relation to the undertaking referred to in section 43(2) above regarding the dispensing of medicines as a registered pharmacist.

1946 c. 81.

1815 c. 194.

(2) Nothing in the provisions of the National Health Service Act 1946 as those provisions are reproduced in this Act affects the rights and privileges conferred by the Apothecaries Act 1815 upon any person qualified under that Act to act as an assistant to any apothecary in compounding and dispensing medicines.

### Disqualification of practitioners

8. Where by virtue of section 42(8) of the National Health Service Act 1946 a person's name was, immediately before the coming into force of this Act, disqualified for inclusion in any list referred to in section 42(1) of that Act, that person's name is disqualified for inclusion in any list referred to in section 46(1) above, until such time as the Tribunal or the Secretary of State directs to the contrary.

Regulations made under section 49 above shall have effect for the purposes of this paragraph.

### Definition of " local authority "

9. The definition of "local authority" in section 128(1) above

1936 c. 49.

1936 c. 50.

includes any joint board constituted under the Public Health Act 1936 or under the Public Health (London) Act 1936 or any enactment repealed by those Acts, or any port health authority constituted under those Acts or under any Act passed before those Acts.

1968 c. 46.

### Sections 3 and 4 of the Health Services and Public Health Act 1968

10.—(1) Notwithstanding the repeal by this Act of section 3 of the Health Services and Public Health Act 1968 (transitional provisions relating to accommodation and treatment of private patients), subsection (2) of that section continues to have the same effect in relation to an undertaking given before 31st March 1969 under section 5 of the National Health Service Act 1946 (accommodation for private

patients) as it had immediately before the coming into force of this
Act.

(2) An undertaking given before the coming into force of section
4(1) of the Health Services and Public Health Act 1968 in respect 1968 c. 46.
of payment under section 4 of the National Health Service Act 1946 1946 c. 81.
(accommodation available on part payment) continues to have the
same effect as it had immediately before the coming into force of
this Act.

### Vehicles under section 33 of the Health Services and Public Health Act 1968

11. The provision of vehicles as mentioned in section 33 of the
Health Services and Public Health Act 1968, and the taking of any
such action as is mentioned in subsection (2) of that section, shall
for the purposes of the National Health Service Act 1946 be treated
as having been included among hospital and specialist services provided under Part II of that Act of 1946 as from its commencement.

### Prevention, care and after-care

12. Any arrangements made under section 28(1) of the National
Health Service Act 1946 by a local health authority which were in
force immediately before 9th September 1968 shall—

(a) so far as they could be made under paragraph 2(1) of
Schedule 8 to this Act, continue to have effect as if so
made ;

(b) so far as they relate to any matters falling within section 3(1)
of the Disabled Persons (Employment) Act 1958, continue 1958 c. 33.
to have effect as if made under that section.

### Saving of amendments

13.—(1) Notwithstanding the repeal by this Act of section 76 and
Part I of Schedule 10 to the National Health Service Act 1946, and
section 57(1) and Schedule 4 to the National Health Service 1973 c. 32.
Reorganisation Act 1973—

(a) the amendments made by Part I of Schedule 10 to that
Act of 1946 to the Voluntary Hospitals (Paying Patients) 1936 c. 17.
Act 1936 and to the Public Health Act 1936, and                        1936 c. 49.

(b) the amendments made by paragraphs 2 to 4, 6 to 9, 40, 44,
45, 48 and 49, 56 and 57, 61, 63 and 64, 68 to 71, 73 to
78, 80 to 83, 86 to 91, 93, 95 and 96, 99, 102, 106 to 109,
111, 122 and 123, 124(1) to (4), 125 to 128, 130 to 134, 136
and 151 and 152 of Schedule 4 to that Act of 1973,

shall continue to have the same effect as they had immediately before
the coming into force of this Act, subject to any amendments made
by this Act.

(2) Nothing in this Act affects the Secretary of State's power under
section 58 of the National Health Service Reorganisation Act 1973
to bring into force paragraph 131 of Schedule 4 to that Act.

### Transfers of property by voluntary organisations

14. Notwithstanding the repeal by this Act of section 23(2) of the
National Health Service (Amendment) Act 1949, section 23(1) of that 1949 c. 93.
Act shall be deemed to have had effect as from 5th July 1948.

*Mental Health Act* 1959

15.—(1) Any regulations under section 7 of the Mental Health Act 1959 in force immediately before 9th September 1968, shall, so far as they could be made under paragraph 2 of Schedule 8 to this Act, have effect as if so made.

(2) Any institution provided under section 97 of the Mental Health Act 1959, or deemed to be so provided when that section came into force, shall be deemed to be provided in pursuance of section 4 above.

1973 c. 32.

*The National Health Service Reorganisation Act* 1973

16.—(1) Nothing in this Act affects any remaining duty of the Secretary of State in connection with the arrangements for the reorganisation of the health service in accordance with section 1 of the National Health Service Reorganisation Act 1973.

(2) The repeal by this Act of section 57(1) of and Schedule 4 to the National Health Service Reorganisation Act 1973 does not affect any exercise of the Secretary of State's powers in relation to that Schedule conferred on him by section 15(3) of that Act.

*Complaints in respect of preserved Boards or bodies abolished under section 14 of the National Health Service Reorganisation Act 1973*

17.—(1) Regulations may provide that where a relevant body within the meaning of section 34 of the National Health Service Reorganisation Act 1973 is abolished by virtue of section 14 of that Act, any prescribed provisions of Part V of this Act and Schedule 13 to this Act shall apply, with or without prescribed modifications, in relation to a complaint which—

(a) was duly made to a Commissioner under Part V before the date of the abolition, or

(b) was made in accordance with the regulations within the period of one year beginning with that date.

(2) For so long as a Board of Governors of a teaching hospital is a preserved Board within the meaning of section 15(6) of the National Health Service Reorganisation Act 1973, that Board of Governors shall be treated as if it were a relevant body for the purposes of Part V of this Act by virtue of section 109 above.

*Permission deemed to have been granted under section 9(5) of the Health Services Act 1976*

1976 c. 83.

18. Where under any arrangements terminated by virtue of section 9(5) of the Health Services Act 1976—

(a) a person was deemed to have been granted under that section permission to use accommodation and facilities to the same extent and for the same purposes as were covered by those arrangements, then

(b) that person shall be deemed to have been granted under section 72 above the like permission (and the provisions of that section shall apply accordingly).

## SCHEDULE 15

CONSEQUENTIAL AMENDMENTS

## ACTS

*The Midwives Act 1936 c.40*

1. In section 2(3) of the Midwives Act 1936, the first reference to that Act shall be construed as including a reference to sections 2 and 3 of this Act.

*The Education Act 1944 c.31*

2. In section 48(4) of the Education Act 1944, for the words " section 3(1) or 3(2)(*a*)(i) of the National Health Service Reorganisation Act 1973 " substitute " section 5(1) of the National Health Service Act 1977 or paragraph 1(*a*)(i) of Schedule 1 to that Act ".

*The Education Act 1946 c.50*

3. In paragraph (*c*) of section 4(2) of the Education Act 1946, for the words " section 3 of the National Health Service Reorganisation Act 1973 " substitute " paragraph (*a*) of section 5(1) of the National Health Service Act 1977 and Schedule 1 to that Act ".

*The Polish Resettlement Act 1947 c.19*

4. In section 4(1) of the Polish Resettlement Act 1947, for the words " National Health Service Act, 1946, or the National Health Service Reorganisation Act 1973 " substitute " National Health Service Act 1977 ", and for the words " those Acts " substitute " that Act ".

*The National Assistance Act 1948 c.29*

5. In paragraph (*c*) of section 21(7) of the National Assistance Act 1948, for the words " National Health Service Acts 1946 to 1973 " substitute " National Health Service Act 1977 ".

6. In paragraph (*b*) of section 29(6) of the National Assistance Act 1948, for the words " National Health Service Act, 1946, the National Health Service Reorganisation Act 1973 " substitute " National Health Service Act 1977 ".

7. In section 47(8) of the National Assistance Act 1948, for the words " National Health Service Act 1946, or the National Health Service Reorganisation Act 1973 " substitute " National Health Service Act 1977 ".

*The Law Reform (Personal Injuries) Act 1948 c.41*

8. In section 2(4) of the Law Reform (Personal Injuries) Act 1948, for the words " National Health Service Act 1946 " substitute " National Health Service Act 1977 ".

*The Children Act* 1948 *c.*43

9. In section 59(1) of the Children Act 1948, in the definition of "hospital", for the words "section seventy-nine of the National Health Service Act, 1946," substitute "section 128(1) of the National Health Service Act 1977".

*The Nurseries and Child-Minders Regulation Act* 1948 *c.*53

10. In section 13(1) of the Nurseries and Child-Minders Regulation Act 1948, in the definition of "hospital", for the words "section seventy-nine of the National Health Service Act 1946," substitute "section 128(1) of the National Health Service Act 1977".

*The National Service Act* 1948 *c.*64

11. In paragraph 3 of Schedule 1 to the National Service Act 1948, for the words "section 12 of the Health Services and Public Health Act 1968" substitute "paragraph 2 of Schedule 8 to the National Health Service Act 1977".

*The Reserve and Auxiliary Forces (Protection of Civil Interests) Act* 1951 *c.*65

12. In Part I of Schedule 2 to the Reserve and Auxiliary Forces (Protection of Civil Interests) Act 1951—

(*a*) in paragraph 15, in the first column, for the words from "Regional" to "1946" substitute "Board of Governors preserved under section 15(1) of the National Health Service Reorganisation Act 1973, or a health authority or other body constituted under the National Health Service Act 1977", and, in the second column, before "The Board", insert "The Authority"; and

(*b*) in paragraph 16, in the first column, for the words "National Health Service Act, 1946" substitute "National Health Service Act 1977" and, in the second column, for the words "The Executive Council" substitute "The Area Health Authority".

*The Landlord and Tenant Act* 1954 *c.*56

13. In section 57(6) of the Landlord and Tenant Act 1954, for the words "National Health Service Act 1946 and the National Health Service Reorganisation Act 1973" substitute "National Health Service Act 1977".

*The Medical Act* 1956 *c.*76

14.—(1) In section 16(1) of the Medical Act 1956, for the words "section 2 of the National Health Service Reorganisation Act 1973" substitute "sections 2 and 3 of the National Health Service Act 1977".

(2) In paragraph (*a*) of subsection (2) of that section, for the words "Part IV of the National Health Service Act 1946" substitute "Part II of the National Health Service Act 1977".

## *The Nurses Act* 1957 *c.* 15

15. In section 13(1) of the Nurses Act 1957, for the words " section 47 of the National Health Service Reorganisation Act 1973 " substitute " section 97 of the National Health Service Act 1977 ".

16. In section 33(1) of the Nurses Act 1957, in the definition of " hospital " for the words " National Health Service Act, 1946 " substitute " National Health Service Act 1977 ", and in the definition of " region ", for the words " National Health Service Reorganisation Act 1973 " substitute " National Health Service Act 1977 ".

17. In paragraph 3(*e*) of Schedule 1 to the Nurses Act 1957, for the words " section 2 of the National Health Service Reorganisation Act 1973 " substitute " sections 2 and 3 of the National Health Service Act 1977 ".

## *The Dentists Act* 1957 *c.* 28

18. In section 42(4) of the Dentists Act 1957, for the words " section 2 or 3 of the National Health Service Reorganisation Act 1973 " substitute " sections 2 and 3 and paragraph (*a*) of section 5(1) and Schedule 1 of the National Health Service Act 1977 ", and for the words " the said sections 2 or Article 5 " substitute " section 2 and section 3 of that Act of 1977 or section 2 of that Act of 1972 or Article 5 of that Order of 1972 ".

## *The Opticians Act* 1958 *c.* 32

19. In paragraph (*b*) of section 21(2) of the Opticians Act 1958, for the words " Part IV of the National Health Service Act, 1946, the National Health Service Reorganisation Act 1973 " substitute " the National Health Service Act 1977 ".

20. In section 30(1) of the Opticians Act 1958—

(*a*) in the definition of " health service ophthalmic lists "—

(i) for the word " supplementary " where it first occurs substitute " general " ;

(ii) for the words " section forty-one of the National Health Service Act 1946 " substitute " section 39 of the National Health Service Act 1977 " ;

(*b*) in the definition of " health service tribunal ", for the words " Seventh Schedule to the said Act of 1946 " substitute " Schedule 9 to the National Health Service Act 1977 ".

## *The Disabled Persons (Employment) Act* 1958 *c.* 33

21. In section 3(2) of the Disabled Persons (Employment) Act 1958, for the words " section twenty-eight of the National Health Service Act, 1946 " substitute " paragraph 2 of Schedule 8 to the National Health Service Act 1977 ".

## *The Public Records Act* 1958 *c.* 51

22. In Part I of the Table in Schedule 1 to the Public Records Act 1958, in the entry relating to the Department of Health and Social Security (formerly the entry relating to the Ministry of Health) after

SCH. 15

the words " National Health Service Reorganisation Act 1973 " add " or section 92 of the National Health Service Act 1977 ", and after the words " said Act of 1973 " add " or section 90 or 91 of the National Health Service Act 1977 ".

*The Mental Health Act* 1959 *c.* 72

23. In section 3(1) of the Mental Health Act 1959, for " National Health Service Reorganisation Act 1973 " substitute " National Health Service Act 1977 ".

24.—(1) In subsection (1) of section 8 of the Mental Health Act 1959, for the words " section twenty-eight of the National Health Service Act 1946 " substitute " paragraph 2 of Schedule 8 to the National Health Service Act 1977 ".

(2) In subsection (2) of that section, for the words " Part III of the National Health Service Act 1946 " substitute " Schedule 8 to the National Health Service Act 1977 ".

(3) In subsection (4) of that section, omit the words " Part III of the National Health Service Act, 1946, and under " and after the words " National Assistance Act, 1948 " add " and under Schedule 8 to the National Health Service Act 1977 ".

25. In section 9(1) of the Mental Health Act 1959, for the words " section twenty-eight of the National Health Service Act, 1946 " substitute " paragraph 2 of Schedule 8 to the National Health Service Act 1977 ".

26. In section 28(3) of the Mental Health Act 1959, for the words " section five of the National Health Service Act, 1946 " substitute " section 65 or section 66 of the National Health Service Act 1977 ".

27. In section 41(3) of the Mental Health Act 1959, for the words " National Health Service Act, 1946 " substitute " National Health Service Act 1977 " and for the words " Part II of that Act " substitute " Part I of that Act ".

28. In section 59(1) of the Mental Health Act 1959, for the words " National Health Service Acts 1946 to 1973 " substitute " National Health Service Act 1977 ".

29. In paragraph (*b*) of section 128(1) of the Mental Health Act 1959, omit the words " the National Health Service Act, 1946, or ", and the words " or the National Health Service Reorganisation Act 1973 " and after the words " National Assistance Act 1948 " insert " or the National Health Service Act 1977 ".

30. In section 133(2) of the Mental Health Act 1959, for the words " National Health Service Act 1946 and the National Health Service Reorganisation Act 1973 " substitute " National Health Service Act 1977 ", and for the words " those Acts " substitute " that Act ".

31. In section 135(6) of the Mental Health Act 1959, for the words " Part I of the Health Services and Public Health Act 1968 " substitute " paragraph 2 of Schedule 8 to the National Health Service Act 1977 ".

32. In section 142(2) of the Mental Health Act 1959, for the words " section fifty-seven of the National Health Service Act 1946 " substitute " section 85 of the National Health Service Act 1977 ".

33. In section 147(1) of the Mental Health Act 1959 (interpretation)—

   (*a*) in the definition of " hospital ", for the words " National Health Service Acts 1946 to 1973 " substitute " National Health Service Act 1977 ", and

   (*b*) in the definition of " special hospital ", for the words " National Health Service Reorganisation Act 1973 " substitute " National Health Service Act 1977 ".

34. In section 154(2) of the Mental Health Act 1959, for the words " subsection (3) of section eighty of the National Health Service Act 1946 " substitute " section 130(4) of the National Health Service Act 1977 ".

### The Health Visiting and Social Work (Training) Act 1962 c.33

35. In sections 3(5) and 5(1) of the Health Visiting and Social Work (Training) Act 1962, for the words " Part III of the National Health Service Act 1946 " substitute in each of those subsections " Schedule 8 to the National Health Service Act 1977 ".

### The National Health Service Act 1966 c.8

36. In section 2(1) of the National Health Service Act 1966, for the words " National Health Service Act 1946 " substitute " National Health Service Act 1977 ".

37. In section 10 of the National Health Service Act 1966—

   (*a*) in subsection (1), for the words " Part IV of the National Health Service Act 1946 " substitute " Part II of the National Health Service Act 1977 ", and in paragraph (*a*) of that subsection for the words " section 43 of the said Act of 1946 " substitute " section 56 of the said Act of 1977 " ;

   (*b*) for subsection (3) substitute—

      " (3) Section 29(4) of the National Health Service Act 1977 shall cease to have effect on the coming into operation of this section."

### The Building Control Act 1966 c.27

38. In paragraph (*h*) of section 5(1) of the Building Control Act 1966, for the words " section 5 of the National Health Service Reorganisation Act 1973 " substitute " sections 8 to 11 of the National Health Service Act 1977 ".

### The General Rate Act 1967 c.9

39. In paragraph (*b*) of section 45 of the General Rate Act 1967, for the words " section 28(1) of the National Health Service Act 1946 " substitute " paragraph 2 of Schedule 8 to the National Health

SCH. 15   Service Act 1977", and for the words "said section 28(1)" substitute "said paragraph 2".

### The Superannuation (Miscellaneous Provisions) Act 1967 c.28

40. In section 7(1) of the Superannuation (Miscellaneous Provisions) Act 1967, in paragraph (a) for the words "National Health Service Acts 1946 to 1973" substitute "National Health Service Act 1977", and in paragraph (b) for "Acts of 1946 to 1973" substitute "Act of 1977".

### The Abortion Act 1967 c.87

41. In section 6 of the Abortion Act 1967, for the words "National Health Service Acts 1946 to 1966" substitute "National Health Service Act 1977".

### The Leasehold Reform Act 1967 c.88

42. In paragraph (c) of section 28(6) of the Leasehold Reform Act 1967, for the words "National Health Service Acts 1946 to 1973" substitute "National Health Service Act 1977".

### The Health Services and Public Health Act 1968 c.46

43. In paragraph (b) of section 45(4) of the Health Services and Public Health Act 1968, for the words "National Health Service Act 1946 or Part I of this Act or the National Health Service Reorganisation Act 1973" substitute "National Health Service Act 1977".

44. In section 59(2) of the Health Services and Public Health Act 1968, for the words "Part IV of the National Health Service Act 1946" substitute "Part II of the National Health Service Act 1977".

45.—(1) In paragraph (b) of section 63(2) of the Health Services and Public Health Act 1968, for the words "Part IV of the 1946 Act" substitute "Part II of the 1977 Act".

(2) In subsection (8) of that section—

(a) for the words ' "1946 Act" means the National Health Service Act 1946' substitute ' "1977 Act" means the National Health Service Act 1977';

(b) in paragraph (a) of the definition of "the relevant enactments" for the words "and Part I of this Act and section 45 thereof" substitute "section 45 of this Act and the National Health Service Act 1977";

(c) in paragraph (b) of the definition of "the relevant enactments" for the words "and Part I of this Act and section 45 thereof and the National Health Service Reorganisation Act 1973" substitute "section 45 of this Act and the National Health Service Act 1977".

46. In section 64(3) of the Health Services and Public Health Act 1968—

(a) omit paragraph (a)(ii);

(b) omit paragraph (a)(xvi);

(c) after paragraph (a)(xvii) add "(xviii) the National Health Service Act 1977."

47. In section 65(3) of the Health Services and Public Health Act 1968—

    (*a*) omit paragraph (*b*)(ii) ;

    (*b*) omit paragraph (*b*)(xvii) ;

    (*c*) after paragraph (*b*)(xviii) add " (xix) the National Health Service Act 1977 ".

### *The Social Work (Scotland) Act* 1968 *c.*49

48. In section 86(3) of the Social Work (Scotland) Act 1968, for " Part II of the National Health Service Act 1946 " substitute " sections 2 and 3 of the National Health Service Act 1977 ".

### *The Medicines Act* 1968 *c.*67

49. In section 131(5) of the Medicines Act 1968, for the words " National Health Service Acts 1946 to 1973 " substitute " National Health Service Act 1977 ".

50. In section 132(1) of the Medicines Act 1968, in the definition of " health centre ", for the words " section 2 of the National Health Service Reorganisation Act 1973 " substitute " section 2 or 3 of the National Health Service Act 1977 ".

### *The Local Authority Social Services Act* 1970 *c.*42

51. In Schedule 1 of the Local Authority Social Services Act 1970, for the entry relating to the National Health Service Act 1946 substitute in the appropriate chronological order—

    (*a*) in the column headed " Enactment ", the words " National Health Service Act 1977 Schedule 8 " ;

    (*b*) in the column headed " Nature of functions ", the words " Care of mothers and young children ; prevention, care and after-care ; home help and laundry facilities "

### *The Vehicles (Excise) Act* 1971 *c.*10

52. In paragraph (*b*) of section 7(2) of the Vehicles (Excise) Act 1971, for the words " section 33(3) of the Health Services and Public Health Act 1968 " substitute " paragraph 2 of Schedule 2 to the National Health Service Act 1977 ".

### *The Tribunals and Inquiries Act* 1971 *c.*62

53. In Part I of Schedule 1 to the Tribunals and Inquiries Act 1971—

    (*a*) in paragraph 17(*a*), for the words " section 5 of the National Health Service Reorganisation Act 1973 " substitute " section 10 of the National Health Service Act 1977 " ;

    (*b*) in paragraph 17(*b*), for the words " section 42 of the National Health Service Act 1946 (c.81) " substitute " section 46 of the National Health Service Act 1977 " ;

    (*c*) in paragraph 17(*c*), for the words " National Health Service Acts 1946 to 1973 " substitute " National Health Service Act 1977 ".

### *The Finance Act* 1971 *c.*68

54. In section 7 of the Finance Act 1971, for the words " National Health Service Act 1946 and the Health Services and Public Health Act 1968 " substitute " National Health Service Act 1977 ".

55. In paragraph 1(1) of Schedule 13 to the Finance Act 1971, for " National Health Service Act 1946 " substitute " National Health Service Act 1977 ".

### *The Road Traffic Act* 1972 *c.*20

56. In paragraph (*a*) of section 156(1) of the Road Traffic Act 1972 for the words " National Health Service Acts 1946 to 1973 " substitute " National Health Service Act 1977 ".

### *The Finance Act* 1972 *c.*41

57. In section 70 of the Finance Act 1972 for the words " section 33(3)of the Health Services and Public Health Act 1968 " substitute " paragraph 2 of Schedule 2 to the National Health Service Act 1977 ".

### *The National Health Service Reorganisation Act* 1973 *c.*32

58. In section 14(2) of the National Health Service Reorganisation Act 1973, for the words " subsection (2) or (3) of section 55 of the principal Act " substitute " subsection (1) or (2) of section 98 of the National Health Service Act 1977 ".

59. In section 15 of the National Health Service Reorganisation Act 1973, after subsection (5) insert the following subsection—

" (5A) So far as may be necessary for the purposes of subsections (3) to (5) above, any reference in those subsections to this Act, or to any instrument in force by virtue of this Act, shall (as the case may be) include a reference to—

(*a*) any provision of this Act which has been repealed and re-enacted by the National Health Service Act 1977 ;

(*b*) any instrument in force by virtue of a provision of this Act which has been repealed and re-enacted by that Act of 1977."

### *The Local Government Act* 1974 *c.*7

60. In paragraph (*b*) of section 29(5) of the Local Government Act 1974, for the words " that section (as applied by section 36 of the National Health Service Reorganisation Act 1973) " substitute " paragraph 16 of Schedule 13 to the National Health Service Act 1977 ".

61. In section 33 of the Local Government Act 1974—

(*a*) in subsection (1), for the words " section 34 of the Act of 1973 " substitute " sections 109, 110, 113, 115 and 116 of the National Health Service Act 1977 ", and for the words " Part III of the Act of 1973 " substitute " Part V of the Act of 1977 " ;

(*b*) in subsection (3), for the words " Part III of the Act of 1973 " in the two places where they occur substitute " Part V of the Act of 1977 " ;

(c) in subsection (4), for the words "Part III of the Act of
1973" substitute "Part V of the Act of 1977";

(d) in subsection (5), for the words "that section as applied
by section 36 of the Act of 1973" substitute "paragraph 16
of Schedule 13 to the Act of 1977";

(e) in subsection (6), for the words 'the "Act of 1973" means
the National Health Service Reorganisation Act 1973' substitute 'the "Act of 1977" means the National Health
Service Act 1977'.

*The Trade Union and Labour Relations Act 1974 c.52*
62. In paragraph (a) of section 30(2) of the Trade Union and
Labour Relations Act 1974, for the words "section 33, section 38,
section 40 or section 41 of the National Health Service Act 1946"
substitute "sections 29, 35, 38 or 41 of the National Health Service
Act 1977".

*The Social Security Act 1975 c.14*
63. In paragraph (a) of section 35(6) of the Social Security Act
1975, for the words "section 12 of the Health Services and Public
Health Act 1968" substitute "paragraph 2 of Schedule 8 to the
National Health Service Act 1977".

64. In paragraph (a) of section 37A(6) of the Social Security Act
1975, for the words "section 33 of the Health Services and Public
Health Act 1968" substitute "paragraph (a) of section 5(2) and
Schedule 2 of the National Health Service Act 1977".

*The House of Commons Disqualification Act 1975 c.24*
65. In Part II of Schedule 1 to the House of Commons Disqualification Act 1975, in the entry relating to the Medical Practices
Committee, for the words "section 34 of the National Health Service
Act 1946" substitute "section 7 of the National Health Service Act
1977".

*The Nursing Homes Act 1975 c.37*
66. In section 2(3) of the Nursing Homes Act 1975—

(a) in paragraph (a), for the words "National Health Service
Act 1946" substitute "National Health Service Act 1977";

(b) in paragraph (b), for the words "National Health Service
Acts 1946 to 1973" substitute "National Health Service
Act 1977";

(c) in paragraph (c), for the words "section 40(1) of the
National Health Service Reorganisation Act 1973" substitute "section 4 of the National Health Service Act 1977".

*The Child Benefit Act 1975 c.61*
67. In paragraph (c) of section 3(3) of the Child Benefit Act 1975,
for the words "section 12 of the Health Services and Public Health
Act 1968" substitute "paragraph 2 of Schedule 8 to the National
Health Service Act 1977".

*The Health Services Act 1976 c.83*
68. In section 2(1) of the Health Services Act 1976, for the words
"Sections 3 to 5 below", substitute "Section 3 below (and sections
68 to 71 of the National Health Service Act 1977)".

69. In section 13(2) of the Health Services Act 1976—

(*a*) in paragraph (*a*), for the words "National Health Service Acts" substitute "National Health Service Act 1977"; and

(*b*) in paragraph (*b*) for the words "those Acts" substitute "that Act".

70. In section 14(5) of the Health Services Act 1976, for the words "National Health Service Acts" substitute "National Health Service Act 1977".

*The Social Security (Miscellaneous Provisions) Act 1977 c.5*

71. In paragraph (*a*) of section 13(3) of the Social Security (Miscellaneous Provisions) Act 1977, for the words "section 33 of the Health Services and Public Health Act 1968" substitute "paragraph (*a*) of section 5(2) and Schedule 2 of the National Health Service Act 1977" and for the words "subsection (3) of that section" substitute "paragraph 2 of that Schedule".

## ORDER

*The Health and Personal Social Services (Northern Ireland)*
*Order 1972 S.I. 1972/1265 (N.I. 14)*

72. In paragraph 7 of Schedule 11 to the Health and Personal Social Services (Northern Ireland) Order 1972 for the words "Part IV of the National Health Service Act 1946" substitute "Part II of the National Health Service Act 1977".

Section 129.

## SCHEDULE 16

Rᴇᴘᴇᴀʟs

| Chapter | Short title | Extent of repeal |
|---|---|---|
| 26 Geo. 5 & 1 Edw. 8. c. 49. | The Public Health Act 1936. | Section 203. |
| 9 & 10 Geo. 6. c. 81. | The National Health Service Act 1946. | The whole Act. |
| 12, 13 & 14 Geo. 6. c. 93. | The National Health Service (Amendment) Act 1949. | Section 8. Sections 10 and 11. Sections 14 to 18. Sections 20(1) and 21. Section 23. Section 25. Sections 28 and 29(1). In section 32(1), the words from "and this Act" where they first occur to "1946 and 1949". In the Schedule, Part I. |
| 14 & 15 Geo. 6. c. 31. | The National Health Service Act 1951. | The whole Act. |
| 15 & 16 Geo. 6. & 1 Eliz. 2. c. 25. | The National Health Service Act 1952. | The whole Act. |

| Chapter | Short title | Extent of repeal |
|---|---|---|
| 7 & 8 Eliz. 2. c. 72. | The Mental Health Act 1959. | In section 8(4), the words " Part III of the National Health Service Act, 1946, and under ". In section 128(1), in paragraph (b), the words " the National Health Service Act, 1946, or ", and the words, " or the National Health Service Reorganisation Act 1973 ". In Schedule 7, the entries relating to the National Health Service Act 1946, and the National Health Service (Amendment) Act 1949. |
| 8 & 9 Eliz. 2. c. 49. | The Public Health Laboratory Service Act 1960. | The whole Act. |
| 9 & 10 Eliz. 2. c. 19. | The National Health Service Act 1961. | The whole Act. |
| 1964 c. 60. | The Emergency Laws (Re-enactments and Repeals) Act 1964. | Section 5. In section 15, the words " the National Health Service Acts 1946 to 1973 ", and the words " and the corresponding enactments of the Parliament of Northern Ireland ". |
| 1965 c. 42. | The Public Health (Notification of Births) Act 1965. | The whole Act. |
| 1966 c. 8. | The National Health Service Act 1966. | In section 12(2), from the words " so far as " where they first occur to the words " and this Act ". |
| 1968 c. 46. | The Health Services and Public Health Act 1968. | Part I. In section 63(8), in paragraph (a) of the definition of " the relevant enactments ", the words " the 1946 Act ". In section 64(3), paragraph (a)(ii) and paragraph (a)(xvi). In section 65(3), paragraph (b)(ii) and paragraph (b)(xvii). In section 79(1), from the words " and the " where they first occur to the words " 1946 to 1968 ". In Schedule 2, Part I. |
| 1968 c. 67. | The Medicines Act 1968. | In Schedule 5, paragraph 11. |
| 1970 c. 42. | The Local Authority Social Services Act 1970. | In Schedule 1, in the entry relating to the Health Services and Public Health Act 1968, the references to sections 12 and 13 in the column headed " Enactment " and in the column headed " Nature of functions ". |

| Chapter | Short title | Extent of repeal |
|---|---|---|
| 1972 c. 70. | The Local Government Act 1972. | In Schedule 23, paragraphs 1, 5, 15(1) and (2). |
| 1973 c. 32. | The National Health Service Reorganisation Act 1973. | Sections 2 to 13.<br>In section 15(3), the words " and in particular nothing in any provision of this Act amending section 55 of the principal Act (which relates to accounts) ".<br>Sections 21 and 22.<br>Section 28.<br>Part III.<br>Section 40.<br>Sections 42 and 43.<br>Sections 45 to 48.<br>Sections 50 to 53.<br>Section 54(1) and (5).<br>In section 55(1), the definitions of " special hospital " and " Special Trustees ".<br>In section 56—<br>(*a*) in subsection (1), in paragraph (*a*), the words " or by virtue of section 34(1)(*h*) or (6) of this Act or subsection (6) of the following section ";<br>(*b*) in subsection (3), the reference " 23(2) ";<br>(*c*) in subsection (4), the words " and any power conferred by section 7 of this Act to give directions by an instrument in writing ";<br>(*d*) in subsection (5), the words " other than section 7 ".<br>In section 57, subsections (1) and (6).<br>In section 58—<br>(*a*) in subsection (1), the word " and " where it first occurs, and paragraph (*a*);<br>(*b*) subsection (6).<br>Schedules 1, 3 and 4. |
| 1974 c. 7. | The Local Government Act 1974. | In Schedule 6, paragraph 21. |
| 1976 c. 48. | The Parliamentary and other Pensions and Salaries Act 1976. | Section 7. |
| 1976 c. 59. | The National Health Service (Vocational Training) Act 1976. | The whole Act. |

| Chapter | Short title | Extent of repeal |
|---------|-------------|------------------|
| 1976 c. 83. | The Health Services Act 1976. | Section 2.<br>Sections 4 and 5.<br>Sections 7 to 11.<br>In section 23—<br>  (*a*) in subsection (1), the definitions of " the 1946 Act " and " the National Health Service Acts ";<br>  (*b*) subsections (3) to (5).<br>In Schedule 1, Part V.<br>Schedule 3.<br>In Schedule 4, Part I. |

## TABLE OF DERIVATIONS

SHOWING THE DERIVATIONS OF THE PROVISIONS OF THE BILL

NOTES:—

1. The following abbreviations are used in this Table:—

1946 = National Health Service Act 1946
    (1946 c. 81)

1949 = National Health Service (Amendment) Act 1949
    (1949 c. 93)

1951 = National Health Service Act 1951
    (1951 c. 31)

1952 = National Health Service Act 1952
    (1952 c. 25)

1960 = Public Health Laboratory Service Act 1960
    (1960 c. 49)

1961 = National Health Service Act 1961
    (1961 c. 19)

1968 = Part I, Health Services and Public Health Act 1968
    (1968 c. 46)

1973 = National Health Service Reorganisation Act 1973
    (1973 c. 32)

1976 = National Health Service (Vocational Training) Act 1976
    (1976 c. 59)

2. The Table does not acknowledge the transfer by the Secretary of State for Social Services Order 1968, S.I. 1968, No. 1699, to the Secretary of State of all the functions of the Minister of Health.

| Clause of Bill | Derivation |
|---|---|
| 1(1) | 1946 s. 1(1); 1973 s. 57 and Sch. 4 para. 10. |
| (2) | 1946 s. 1(2); Health Services Act 1976 c. 83 s. 23(3). |
| 2 | 1973 s. 2(1). |
| 3(1) | 1973 s. 2(2). |
| (2) | 1946 s. 61. |
| (3) | 1973 s. 2(3). |
| 4 | 1973 s. 40(1). |
| 5(1) | 1973 ss. 3(1), 4. |
| (2) | 1946 ss. 16, 17; 1951 s. 3; 1960 s. 5(2); 1968 s. 33(1); 1973 s. 57 and Sch. 4 paras. 14, 15, 97. |
| (3) | 1946 s. 3(3); 1973 s. 57 and Sch. 4 para. 12(2). |
| (4) | 1960 s. 1(1), 5(2). |
| (5) | 1960 s. 1(1). |
| 6(1) | 1946 s. 2(1); 1973 s. 57 and Sch. 4 para. 11. |
| (2) | 1946 s. 2(1), (2), (6). |
| (3) | 1946 s. 2(3). |
| (4) | 1946 s. 2(3). |
| (5) | 1946 s. 2(4). |
| (6) | 1946 s. 2(5). |
| (7) | 1946 s. 2(5) proviso. |